Healing and Empowering the Feminine

A LABYRINTH JOURNEY

Sylvia Shaindel Senensky

Chiron Publications
Wilmette, Illinois

Printed at McNaughton & Gunn Inc.
Cover design by D. J. Hyde
Interior design by Sans Serif Inc.

ISBN: 1-888602-26-0

Credits:
pp. xi, 25, 119, and 151: From John Moyne and Coleman Barks, *Unseen Rain: Quatrains of Rumi.* Originally published by Threshold Books.
pp. 14, 20 (right): Figures 298 and 299 [p. 193] from THE LANGUAGE OF THE GODDESS by MARIJA GIMBUTAS. Copyright © 1989 by Marija Gimbutas. Reprinted by permission of HarperCollins Publishers Inc.
p. 17: Layard, John. "The Malekulan Journey of the Dead," *Eranos Yearbooks.* Bollingen Series XXII. Copyright © 1960 by Princeton University Press. Reprinted by permission of Princeton University Press.
pp. 86–87: Whitmont, Edward C. *The Symbolic Quest—Basic Concepts of Analytical Psychology.* Copyright © 1969 by C. G. Jung Foundation, © 1970 by Princeton University Press. Reprinted by permission of Princeton University Press.
p. 137: Excerpt from "The Weighing" from THE OCTOBER PALACE by JANE HIRSHFIELD. Copyright © 1994 by Jane Hirshfield. Reprinted by permission of HarperCollins Publishers Inc.
pp. 155–158: From INANNA: LADY OF THE LARGEST HEART: POEMS OF THE HIGH PRIESTESS ENHEDUANNA by Betty De Shong Meador, Copyright © 2000. By permission of the author and the University of Texas.
pp. 173, 182, 186–187: Selected lines from "Transcendental Etude," "Hunger," "Natural Resources," "Splittings," and "Upper Broadway", from THE DREAM OF COMMON LANGUAGE: Poems 1974–1977 by Adrienne Rich. Copyright © 1978 by W. W. Norton & Company, Inc. Used by permission of the author and W. W. Norton & Company, Inc.
p. 179: Part II of "Sources", from YOUR NATIVE LAND, YOUR LIFE: Poems by Adrienne Rich. Copyright © 1986 by Adrienne Rich. Used by permission of the author and W. W. Norton & Company, Inc.
p. 181: "For strong women" by Marge Piercy © 1977, 1982 by Marge Piercy and Middlemarsh, Inc. From *Circles on the Water,* published by Alfred A. Knopf, Inc. First appeared in Chrysalis #4, 1977. Used by permission of Wallace Literary Agency.

To my grandmothers
> Shaindel Devorah Barnbaum Shtilwasser
> Dora Pinskwer Senensky

To my mother
> Anne Betty Stillwater Senensky

*To all those who courageously choose to live their lives
from a place deeply connected to their authentic
feminine selves*

CONTENTS

Preface   vii
Acknowledgments   xi
Introduction—Walking the Labyrinth   1

PART I: **About the Labyrinth**

1: Roots of the Labyrinth   15
The Archetypal Dimension   20
The Labyrinth as "Planned Chaos"   22

2: The Labyrinth as Symbol   27
As a Spiritual Container   28
As the Rhythm of Soul and Life   32
As Goddess of the Moon   33
As the Way   34
As Ancestral Line   35
As Temenos, Container, and Alchemical Vessel   37
As Initiation Process   37
As Body of the Great Mother   38
As Organs of the Body   39
As the Center, the Mandala   40
As Fortress   41
As Dance   42
As Movement of the Snake   42
As Altered State of Consciousness   44
As Choice   44
As a Game   45

3: The Labyrinth at Chartres   49
The Labyrinth   53
The Center: Aphrodite's Flower   55
Numbers   55
The Ritual   58

PART II: **The Labyrinth: A Journey into the Feminine**

4: The Labyrinth Journey   61
Descent: The Mythic Archetypal Level   65
Regression: The Psychological Level   67
The Call, Allies and Guardians at the Threshold   71

The Journey In   74
The Center   74
Leaving the Center   77
The Way Out   78

5: Reflections on the Feminine   85
The Primordial Feminine   86
The Feminine and Inertia   91
The Archetypal Feminine   94
The Divine Feminine   95
Knowing the Feminine   97
The Feminine Ignored   98
Finding Our Voices   102
The Feminine and Sorrow   105
Understanding the Dark   109
More Dreams of the Feminine   112

PART III: Myths and Fairy Tales of the Journey

Overview   123

6: Theseus and the Minotaur   127
The Theseus Story   128
The Wisdom in the Myth   130
Nicole's Story   134

7: Demeter and Persephone   139
The Persephone Story   140
The Wisdom of the Myth   143

8: Inanna   153
The Inanna Story   159
The Wisdom of the Myth   162

9: Vassilisa the Beautiful   173

Epilogue   181
The Challenge   183
Women in the Peace Process   184
Bibliography   188
Index   192

The labyrinth at Chartres Cathedral.

PREFACE

Dramatic events in the outer world have punctuated the writing of this book. September 11, 2001, occurred just as I was finishing the original manuscript and now, in 2003, we are in the aftermath of a war at least a quarter of the population of this planet tried to prevent.

The shock of the terrorist attacks in North America broke through any illusion we had of being safe. We became aware of the relentless grief, rage, and fear innumerable people on our planet live with on an ongoing basis. It caused many of us to begin to see the world through different eyes and to question why such a thing could happen. What is the meaning of it for us, for our planet, and what lessons are we to learn?

The society from which the terrorists have come is one in which women, and therefore the Feminine, have been demeaned, belittled, disempowered, tortured, and abused. It gives us a compelling and potent example of what happens when the Masculine is disconnected from its Feminine source, particularly that of the Dark Feminine. When the killing of innocent children in a war about power is named as collateral damage, and there is no compassion for life or human suffering, we know something is very wrong. Instead of being ruled by their hearts and the sacredness of all life, we have people in power ruled by an ideology divorced from any feeling other than fanaticism.

At the outbreak of the war on Iraq, an American woman had the following dream.

> I am walking through a hip-deep morass of toxic sludge, holding a baby up as high above as I possibly can. The colors are grey, and people with their backs turned away are urinating and defecating on the pillars that lined the street . . . except for the child, who is the beautiful pink of health, innocence, and hope. I couldn't see what was ahead, but I knew I was moving in the right direction. I felt totally determined to get through it. Even

though I am holding the child up with my arms upraised as far as possible, I don't feel any sense of getting tired. I just keep on walking.

These powerful images give us a graphic depiction of the state of our planet where everything is grey and people are urinating and defecating in public. Within the horror we find hope both in the form of the healthy pink baby, and in the person of the woman who is capable of carrying the baby above the sludge without getting tired. She knows she is walking in the right direction.

The labyrinth journey is an internal one that grounds us in the depth of who we are and helps us to embrace both the dark and light aspects of our human nature. It particularly connects us to the Feminine qualities of our being, for the labyrinth comes to us from the caves of the Great Goddess. There we are aligned with the unremitting rhythm of birth and death, and the sanctity of *all life*.

We have come to a time when we can no longer remain silent. We are being called upon by the sorrowing and powerful Dark Feminine to know our own darkness and the profound richness of all dark places, even when they are laden with pain. Through her we know the mystery of existence and the sacredness of the cycles of life. We learn how important the destruction of the old ways is to the rebirth of the new. When she steps into our lives and awakens us, we can be shattered to our core, and we know, as we see the tears streaming down her face, that she too is holding us in her compassionate and loving embrace.

We need to know her as the source of life in the material realm, and to know her sorrow at how we have so unconsciously set out to destroy her . . . our Mother Earth. She is calling upon us, each in our own way to do our inner work, to become her allies, to become the best human beings we know how to be; to allow our creativity, our compassion, and our love to flow to ourselves and to all life forms on this planet. This is the lesson of the Feminine we all need to remember. We need to honor our earth and all creatures, human and other, that she supports. We need to nourish ourselves, each other, all children, and the unbelievable creative potential within each human being.

I have great hope. Never before have so many had this perspective, and never before have we been able to communicate this knowing to each other so easily and quickly. As we come to a place of love and compassion for ourselves, our struggles, and our own vulnerable humanity, we will at the same time begin to kindle a similar compassion for others. Love attracts love. If we flood our planet with loving and transformative energy, our actions will begin to mirror our feelings. We will come home to ourselves.

> Keep walking, though there's no place to get to.
> Don't try to see through the distances.
> That's not for human beings. Move within,
> but don't move the way fear makes you move.[1]
> —*Rumi*

---

1. John Moyne and Coleman Barks, *Unseen Rain: Quatrains of Rumi*, p. 20.

ACKNOWLEDGMENTS

When a journey to write a book spans a period of fifteen years, many people have gifted me with their stories, insight, and support. I would like to name here those who have been directly involved in the making of this book. My thanks go to all of you, both seen and unseen.

It has been an honor for me to accompany the men and women, who by trusting in the process, have courageously undertaken their personal journey to their transformative centers. The labyrinth container held us as we explored these unknown, sometimes frightening, often illuminating places. We have each been enriched by the experience. I thank you for giving me permission to use your dreams and stories in this book.

I thank Robin Van Doren, who has always seen the possible and held the space for me to move into it, and my wonderful sisters in Women with Wings: Dianna Butler, Patricia Brenninkmeijer Ziel, Patricia Dunbar, Tree Dunbar, Seena Frost, Sharon Hall, Delores Houle, Miriam Kanev, the late Marje Minger, Fran Rothman, Sarah Sadler, and Kathleen Schanz. Together we have journeyed into the unknown, supported, challenged, and loved each other. This book could not have happened if you hadn't spurred me to keep on going when I lost faith, and challenged me to go ever deeper into my knowing.

A special thanks and appreciation to all those who have been teachers and mentors along the path: Jean Houston, Peggy Nash Rubin, Gaye Luce, David Patten, Ursula Wirtz, Catherine Moreau, John Hill, Ursula Ulmer, Kathrin Asper, Connie Steiner, Freya Bleibler, the late Dr. Lois Plumb, and Marion Woodman.

To those who read various versions of the manuscript and engaged me in dialogue about my ideas, I am truly grateful: Virginia Apperson, Barbara Susan Booth, Sharon Butala, Shoshana Cooper, Michael Dean, Patricia Dunbar, Geraldine Fogerty, Betty Kaser, Marilyn Melville, Anna Miransky, Barb Quinlan, and Austin Repath.

Thank you so much for those who have so generously given me permission to use their poetry: Melinda Burns, Pesha Gertler, Dianne Joyce, Jayelle Lindsay, Kathleen Norris, Jennifer Paine Welwood, and Lois Zachariah.

Special thanks to Dianne Brassolotto for her initial editing of the manuscript.

My final thanks goes to my beloved Roger Middleton, whose unending love and support, editing help, and willingness to carry more than his share of household tasks so that I could be freed up to write, made this all possible.

Sylvia Shaindel Senensky
Toronto
May, 2003

Sylvia Senensky, B.OT., M. Ed. is a Zurich-trained Jungian analyst and a graduate of Jean Houston's training program in the Cultivation of Human Capacities. She has lectured internationally on the labyrinth and its connection to the Feminine as well as having twenty-five years experience as a workshop leader. The workshops range from labyrinth walks to the enactment of fairy tales and myths. In all cases ritual, art, music, movement, and sacred dance are used to create a safe container in which participants have the opportunity to understand the archetypal dimension of these stories and deepen their personal relationship to them. Her analytical practice is in Toronto Canada.

Readers are invited to visit the author's website:
www.sylviasenensky.com

Labyrinth in park, Canada.

INTRODUCTION

"The labyrinth has always been the master-pattern of dreams where people have drawn upon a fluid syntax far more ancient than the convolutions of language. To whomever can decipher it, paths of wisdom are revealed therein. It teaches human beings to behold their destiny in one glance, as one holds a wounded bird in the palm of one's hand. It enables them constantly to plumb the depths of their own secrets— and to remember them in order to live."[1]

—Jacques Attali

The labyrinth is about story. It is a story that takes us back tens of thousands of years to a time when the Great Goddess reigned, when the Feminine was revered and honored, and the mysteries of birth, death, and rebirth were ritualized and regarded with awe. According to Attali, "The imagination of the eighty billion human beings who preceded us on this planet over the last three million

---

1. Jacques Attali, *The Labyrinth in Culture and Society,* p. xxii.

years" is held in the labyrinth story, and when we walk it we know we are walking in the footsteps of our ancestors. The ritual is ancient, the stories held there profound, and their messages are crucial to us as we move into this new millennium with a desire to heal ourselves and our planet.

Those ancient peoples hold for us clues about a part of ourselves—the chaotic, unpredictable, dark, sensual, sexual, seemingly illogical, sometimes frightening, sometimes overwhelming, powerfully energetic, supposedly uncontrollable forces that as a species, particularly in the last 6,000 years, we have put every effort into subduing. This powerful force, which we have come to call the Feminine, is present in both men and women, and both men and women have borne the brunt of the hammer of repression and devastation.

Because I am a woman, and I know this story from within my own body, I am able to speak about it with a certain authenticity. I can listen to the stories of other women from a place of knowing inside myself that echoes their stories and both our stories become larger because of this sharing.

I cannot do the same for men. I believe men's stories to be different from women's and I do not want to speak about something I cannot "know" in the deepest sense of that word. I don't want to presume because I have some understanding of this phenomenon in women, that I must also understand it in men. The pain of that kind of arrogance of knowing turned upon women has been too great, and I will not perpetuate it. Having said that, however, I believe that by learning about the nature of the Feminine energy that resides in all of us, men will learn more about both themselves and the women in their lives.

This book is about the labyrinth as a container for holding the stories of present-day women as we struggle to unravel the opus of our lives in an attempt to understand the complexity of who we are. How often do we find ourselves perplexed by the depth of our feelings and the enigma of our inner images? How often do we respond with an emotional intensity and not know where it came from? We may find ourselves mired in a deep depression with no clue as to its cause and little hope of emerging from it. We may find ourselves acting spontaneously in ways totally out of character with who we think we are. We may be haunted by disturbing images in our dreams. We may know that there is something profound missing and not know where to look for it.

We may have had mothers who, because they too were not able to live from the depth of their true Feminine nature, became negative, controlling, and judgmental toward us. Through a complexity of inner psychic processes we internalized those voices, believing them to hold the "truth," and as a result have treated ourselves as flawed human beings. In order not to pass this negativity along to our daughters, be they of our bodies or not, and in order to heal the planet and Mother Earth, it is the work of our time to reclaim, within each of our stories, the power of the unknown and chaotic Feminine.

I would like to share with you two stories that have formed the ground of this book. Both of them occurred during a three-year training program called "The Cultivation of Human Capacities," directed by Jean Houston, her husband Bob Masters, Robin Van Doren, and Gay Luce, that I attended prior to my training in Zurich as a Jungian Analyst. A hundred and thirty people gathered for two two-week sessions a year for three years in a camp in lower New York State. These two stories were like the bookends of my time in training, occurring in the first and last sessions. In the first session, I was exposed to the labyrinth. In the last session, I connected with a level of Feminine power within myself that astonished me. These two experiences with their mystery, complexity, depth, and power, as well as their connection to each other and to the unfolding story of women's discovery of themselves, inform this work.

The first session of the Human Capacities program took place in January of 1987. My arrival was a true heroine's journey. I traversed the 500 miles from my home near Toronto to the camp in lower New York State during the first and worst blizzard of the season. There were times when we couldn't see the road and were driving on faith alone. The normal nine-hour journey took us sixteen hours. At its end I found myself in a group of strangers, all of whom seemed to know each other, and many of whom were excited about the labyrinth.

For years Jean had used the labyrinth at Chartres, calling it the Dromenon (Greek—"that which is done"), as a symbol of her work. She and her students had frequented the Cathedral at Chartres, annoyed the management by removing the chairs covering the labyrinth there, and danced it many times. Never before had anyone tried to re-create the Chartres labyrinth so it could actually be walked in North America.

Using a diagram, some members of our group went out into a large, empty field and, in the snow left by the same blizzard that had challenged my arrival, created the pattern. It was almost dusk by the time they finished, and the whole group assembled in hushed anticipation of what would come next. The air crackled with awe (in the true sense of the word). Frank, the man who had directed the patterning, reached forward with one arm, and with a voice trembling with emotion asked us to form a line, join hands, and follow him. Jean fell in first, ringing her Druid bell into the stillness of the night.

We couldn't see where we were going but we blindly and trustingly followed those in front of us, listening to the crunch of snow beneath our boots and the delicate but piercing tinkle of the bell. We wound forward and back, in and out, passing others in the snakelike chain. Sometimes we felt squeezed, sometimes we felt the openness of being on the outside of the circle. Sometimes we waited for the end of the chain to come through so we could go on. We knew when we reached the center. There was a shiver of recognition. We didn't stay there this time but moved on, following the rhythmic snake and retracing our steps until we again reached the outside of the sacred circle.

We were in sacred space and mythic time. The archetypal ancestral layer of our psyches was being touched as we participated in the ancient ritual. Although there were not many words that night, there was a knowing that something had been constellated between us and this ancient symbol.

We made our way into the warm gymnasium, and lying on the floor, allowed the experience to permeate and register in our mind–body systems. I could feel a tingling in my brain and could almost retrace the labyrinth pattern as the tingling sensation moved around. It was awesome, beyond anything I had ever expected. My curiosity and longings were aroused. What was this all about? What had happened to us? What was constellated? What were we tapping into? What was the mystery? (A year after this, Dr. Lauren Artress attended one of Jean's workshops, encountering the labyrinth for the first time. Artress went on in her work at Grace Cathedral, San Francisco, to bring about the labyrinth's resurgence into contemporary life.)

The labyrinth continued to haunt me as I moved on in my life. During my training in Zurich it was a presence demanding to be explored further. It became a symbol of the journey of individuation as described by C. G. Jung and evolved into my graduate thesis.

The other bookend occurred in the sixth and final session of the Human Capacities program, and in the opposite season. It was a summer day in late June and because of the profusion of melting snow and heavy spring rain, the river, normally dry by that time of year, still flowed gently over its rocky river bed. The sun was shining and the trees were showing a canopy of green as leaves unfurled and grew, to create shade for the coming heat of summer.

It was just after the tragedy in Tiananmen Square, China, where student protesters were mercilessly killed by the government. Working with a young Chinese woman, Jean was trying to see if this woman could envision what new myth was trying to be born in her troubled country. The woman, struggling with the task, kept getting stuck in her personal story. Jean, gifted in the use of spontaneous ritual to empower, suggested that we go down to the river, and those of us who chose to could lie in the water. The water was to symbolize the Tao—the flow of time moving through us. We would then see what might emerge.

Perhaps it was my naiveté that allowed me to approach this event in a childlike manner. It never occurred to me that an archetypal power could be released, and therefore I felt no fear. At first it was fun to get into the water with all our clothes on. I had never before done that. The water was very shallow and cold, and it was thrilling to lower myself onto the stones, feel the water flow around my body and my clothes become soggy and heavy. At first we played and joked.

Amidst the sound of laughter, I became aware of crying. A small group of us was downstream and away from the rest. A friend lying next to me was in distress and a group gathered around her, supporting her process by putting their hands on her various chakras (energy centers in the body). I went over to join them, placing my hand on her belly, her second chakra. In a very short time I found tears running down my face and motioned for someone to take my place as I moved even further downstream.

Lying on my belly in the cold water, what had begun as gentle tears turned into a torrent. Another friend let me know she was with me by gently touching my shoulder and keeping her hand there throughout the process. Letting the salt of my tears mingle with the clear mountain water, I found I could not stop crying. At first I was flooded with images of personal grief—a friend had died of cancer a few months previously, a relationship I had been in for several years had broken up, it was the last session of an experience that had changed my life—but soon, all images were gone, and deep, heart-wrenching sobs wracked my body. I felt as if I were pouring out the sorrow of millennia into the river of Time and that the sorrow had no end.

Shivering with cold, and still unable to stop crying, I managed to drag myself from the water onto the sun-baked grass. Now, I gifted the earth with my tears until gradually, after what felt like an eternity, the sobs subsided.

Turning over on my back, I saw that a group had gathered around me. As I tried to put words to what was happening, an almost impossible task, a rush of volcanic rage filled the space left by the tears. With the encouragement and safety created by these friends, I was able to surrender to what came next. The screams that emerged were full of unrepentant rage, a searing agony, and a despairing impotence that I was told later could be heard all around the camp. They seemed to come from an uncomprehending depth, swimming in a sea of anguish. They felt like all women's tears and rage. I felt as if I were being purged and purified, and that the emotions were my mother's and my grand-mother's and their mothers' and grandmothers' and all children's mothers' and grandmothers' going back, back, into time.

What happened for me on that summer day was that my heart, which I realize now had felt closed and hard until then, opened. It revealed a hitherto unknown inner world with an underlying ago-nizing quandary: How could human beings willingly, knowingly, and intentionally cause pain to other human beings when there was already so much suffering on our planet beyond our control? I have since discovered that the first rule of the Egyptian Goddess Maat, the Goddess of Justice is "No one should cause pain to others." The second rule is that "No one should make anyone sorrowful."[2]

Over the next few days, my initial exhaustion and emptiness were slowly replaced by a new kind of energy. It was an energy different from anything I have experienced before or since and, as a result, was difficult to articulate. There is a book I read many years ago with an image in it of an "eleven-mile-high dancer." That is how I felt. With my long legs and giant strides I could dance over the earth, creating a great wind as I twirled. I felt in-credibly alive and filled with an indescribable power. I felt huge, strong, and ruthless, but also frightened. I could do anything, but could I stop myself or could anyone stop me?

With the coming of that question came an opportunity to test it out. In a process devised by Jean, the men were to stand in a circle facing outward and the women were to choose a man and, stand-ing in front of him, look him in the eye and connect from our depths. Waiting my turn, my body could not stop moving. As I let the power come into me, I danced round and round the room. I chose the one man I thought would be able to meet me if I let this power show, and when I was ready, went to stand in front of him. To my horror, all I could see was terror in his eyes. I backed away from him, out of the circle, away from the process and found my-self standing face to face with David, a teacher who had joined the program after it had begun. I don't know how I got there. David

2. Marion Woodman, *Dancing in the Flames*, p. 54.

knew the labyrinth. He had walked it since he was a child and walked it in his imagination all the time. He knew where I was coming from, a place that was also inside himself. He was not afraid. He looked me in the eye and said, "You are beautiful. This energy is beautiful." We walked around and around the circle together, his arm around my shoulders as he continued to utter the refrain, "You are beautiful. . . . It is beautiful."

That is what was needed. This Feminine energy in me needed to be met, known, and honored by Masculine energy. My intuition had been right in leading me to stand in front of a man for I sensed that it needed to be met by its opposite. Since then I have learned that although meeting the Masculine energy outside ourselves is very important, meeting the Masculine within is crucial. The Masculine energy helps to give form and shape to what was previously formless and shapeless. It helps to direct Feminine energy when necessary, to make it more accessible, knowable, and therefore a power that can be constructively used.

That entire experience has stayed with me like a lost child seeking to be found. It has kept knocking on the door saying, "Explore me, know me, understand me." Each time I read the writings of women who spoke to this dark Feminine power (Barbara Hannah, Linda Fierz David, Claire Douglas, Adrienne Rich), I breathed a sigh of relieved recognition and quickly copied it down. The end of my graduate thesis for the Jung Institute in Zurich is full of these quotes. I began to realize that this was a power from within the body, born of suffering, of the intimate knowledge of birth and the inevitability of death, of ruthlessness and anguish, of ecstasy and passion. I believe I met the energy of the archetypal dark Feminine that day and I have been asking questions and searching for ways to reconnect ever since.

I see now that the true labyrinthine journey is to connect with the depths of our Feminine essence, to know life both within and without from this core place, and to be able to dance the labyrinth of our lives with the integrity and passion that this knowing allows. No longer are we bothered with wanting power over others, for we are filled with a power from within ourselves that wants to be engaged, known, nourished, and loved. Then it is free to become another strong voice of fierce compassion in our ailing but beautiful world.

Walking the Labyrinth

As I was in the process of writing this book, we received permission from the city of Toronto to paint a fifty-six-foot labyrinth on a round concrete slab surrounded by picnic tables. This slab, formerly the base of a carousel, had been in a large public park near my home for more than sixty years. It is located in a wonderful spot surrounded by groves of trees and indigenous plants. It felt sacred even before we installed the labyrinth and gave the impression that it had been waiting for us to paint it there. One of the paths to the labyrinth takes me through a natural wooded area of the park, and made it a wonderful, grounding pilgrimage for me while writing.

I had never before had the opportunity to walk the labyrinth whenever I chose and it became an integral part of my process. I walked it almost every day. If my thoughts were muddled, it helped clear them. If I had a question, it got answered. If there was something I had neglected to say, it would come to me. If I felt frustrated, it would calm me. If I felt lethargic, it energized me.

Slowly a knowing of the different aspects of the Feminine emerged. I began to sense a compassionate Divine Feminine presence that held me in her loving embrace each time I stepped into the labyrinth. At the same time, with each step I took, I felt a connection back in time to the caves of ancient peoples and their Goddess. I went to those caves in my imagination, and allowed a knowing of the Primordial Feminine energy that reigned there to fill and inform me. I could almost sense it pulsing up through the earth. It became clear that by walking the labyrinth path I was allowing those two energies, that of the Divine Feminine and the Primordial Feminine, to become conscious in me and to intermingle. I knew that I could only safely access the primal level of the Feminine if I allowed myself to be held in the compassionate embrace of the Divine Feminine. We need both these energies, and they need us, in order that they can become manifest in our lives.

Since September 11th my walking of the labyrinth has become even more profound. I can feel Her anguish at the unbearable suffering on our planet. I feel Her rage that we are disconnected from Her, knowing the sacredness of all life, yet allowing this suffering to continue. I feel Her deeply compassionate love holding us, as we bumble along trying to learn how to be human.

Both the Divine and Primordial aspects of the Feminine voice are longing to be heard and known. She is inviting us into Her world that we may be able to dissipate our fear of Her. We need to know Her and love Her in all Her dimensions so that we can know and love those aspects of ourselves. I am deeply honored that I have been given this opportunity to give voice to some part of the knowing of Her and I hope it will also resonate for you in your life.

This book was birthed to unravel threads of a story whose telling may help birth you into your knowing of this mysterious domain. Because none of this is linear, this book could not be written in a linear way. Believe me I tried! It didn't work. When I finally "got it," I was at last free to let the labyrinth tell the story in its own way. When we walk the labyrinth, we go over the same ground many times but always at a different angle, or facing a different direction, or after having traversed some pathways already. We sometimes take great strides forward, only to find ourselves returning to where we have already been. At other times, we seem to move back and forth in small spaces. We never know who or what we will meet on the path. The unexpected is always present. Therefore I encourage you to read this book in whatever way presents itself to you and trust that just as in walking the labyrinth, you will know and understand what you need to.

Remember, the labyrinth is walked twice . . . once in and once out . . . covering the same ground but from a different perspective. Most important, however, on the walk back out you are changed because you have spent time in the center.

To assist you in this process, I have divided the book into three sections. Part I, "About the Labyrinth," will introduce you to the labyrinth, its roots, its symbolic meaning in general, and the more specific significance of the Chartres labyrinth. Part II, "The Labyrinth: A Journey into the Feminine," will explore the nature of the labyrinth journey, and will be followed by reflections on the nature of the Feminine. The final section, III, "Myths and Fairy Tales of the Journey," will be an exploration of the myths of Theseus and the Minotaur, Demeter and Persephone, Inanna, the fairy tale Vassilisa the Beautiful, and their relationship to the labyrinth journey.

I wish you well on this journey of healing and discovery. May it feed your Soul!

PART I:

About the Labyrinth

CHAPTER ONE: Roots of the Labyrinth
CHAPTER TWO: The Labyrinth as Symbol
CHAPTER THREE: The Labyrinth at Chartres

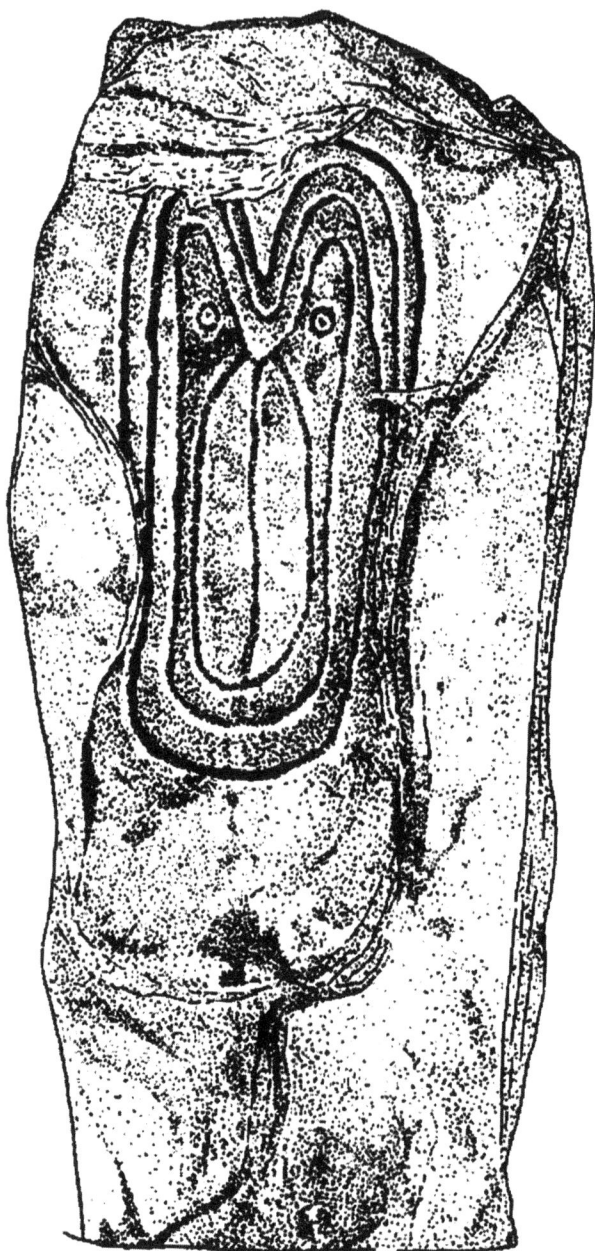

Owl-faced image from grave stela, County Meath, Ireland.

1

ROOTS OF THE LABYRINTH

> *In prehistoric times the cavern, often resembling, or ritually transformed into, a labyrinth, was at once a theatre of initiation and a place where the dead were buried. The labyrinth in its turn, was homologised with the body of the Earth-Mother. To penetrate into a labyrinth or a cavern was the equivalent of a mystical return to the Mother.*[1]
>
> —Mircea Eliade

There is a mystery surrounding labyrinths. Whether we walk them or use them as symbolic tools, we are intrigued and drawn in. Where do labyrinths come from? Who designed them? How and why have they evolved over the ages? Why are they so numinous?

Many wonderful books have been written on the history of labyrinths, their locations around the planet, and their use as tools for meditation and the creation of ritual (see the Bibliography at the end of this book). Our focus here is the labyrinth and its deep

1. Mircea Eliade, *Myths, Dreams, and Mysteries*, p. 171.

connection to our roots in the caves of the Earth Mother and its connections to the Feminine.

What do I mean when I use the word *Feminine?* The Feminine is about process and relationship. It is about playing, experimenting, doing several things at once. It is not goal-oriented, although there may be a goal toward which we are heading. It is the process of getting to the goal that is all important. The Feminine can appear illogical when we look at it from the perspective of the Masculine, but it has an inner logic that is its alone. The twists and turns, the forward and backward movement of the labyrinth, the dancing between quadrants, the act of allowing the unexpected to affect your journey, the still point of the center—that is static and containing while honoring the rhythms and movement of life and death—all form an exquisite portrayal of how Feminine energy manifests itself.

The Masculine, on the other hand, heads straight toward its goal. It is decisive and direct, cutting through that which it perceives as extraneous to get to the core. It is active, logical, and linear while working on the premise of cause and effect. Both Masculine and Feminine are necessary and both must be honored.

For 20,000 years, the cave was the home of the Great Goddess. She was found in the most secret recesses, and the journey to find her was labyrinthine. Pilgrims would travel long distances within the caves, and go through cavernous rooms whose ceilings were sometimes cathedral-like in height. Those who have had the privilege of going into the caves in the Dordogne region of southern France have been awed by the Paleolithic art work leading to, and found deep within the inner sanctum of the Goddess. Not only were labyrinths drawn outside caves indicating the path in, they were the paths to the Goddess herself and she resided in their center.

I remember my own journey to Crete, where I had the opportunity to visit caves whose history of use extended back to Paleolithic times. They were mysterious, frightening, and awesome in their grandeur. The sound of water dripping, the little pockets of light high in the ceiling, the musty smell and slippery floor, and moving through spaces on my hands and knees to find myself suddenly in a space so large I could not see the ceiling, all contributed to the wonder of the experience. I imagined ancient peoples wandering in these labyrinthine recesses, coming upon magnificent and gigantic stalagmites and stalactites that were often in the recognizable shape of known animals and luminous from imbedded mineral matter. I could understand the reverence with which they would approach these natural phenomena and how these configurations must have been seen as gifts or messages from an unknowable source.

The cave was the first place of safety and spiritual worship. To prehistoric people it represented the body of the Great Mother into which they could crawl. The rituals that took place within were concerned with birth, death, and rebirth. The caves were the first burial grounds where bodies of the deceased were given back to the Great Mother for safekeeping and resurrection. There were rituals that took place at the mouth of the cave and others that took place in the deeper recesses.

Malekula is an island in the New Hebrides. Its people's funeral rites give us some insight into what might have taken place in those prehistoric times. We are told that at the entrance to the cave, where life meets death, sits Le-Hev-Hev, the Great Goddess in her death aspect. She traces a geometric figure (labyrinth) in the sand. The dead man (initiate) sees her from a distance. He approaches the Devouring Ghost Le-Hev-Hev and she erases half the design. The dead man, whose task it was to memorize these designs in his waking life, must be able to complete the design she has erased. If he is successful, he is able to pass on into the cave and the afterlife. If not, he is devoured by Le-Hev-Hev and his existence ends.[2] (See the artwork opening Chapter 2.)

Some examples of early labyrinths from French excavations follow on pages 19–20.

The two labyrinth patterns most commonly being built and worked with today as tools for meditation are the seven-circuit or Cretan-style labyrinth and the eleven-circuit or Chartres-style labyrinth. We don't know who created the labyrinth designs to

2. John Layard, *The Malekulan Journey of the Dead.*

Seven-circuit Cretan labyrinth.   Eleven-circuit Chartres labyrinth.

begin with, but it is clear that their complexity has grown over the centuries from the simple cave drawings, to the seven-circuit Cretan labyrinth, to the highly complex Chartres labyrinth.

We could hypothesize that the more complex labyrinths of today mirror the complexities of the psyches of modern-day humans, whereas the less complex psyches of our ancestors were mirrored in the more simple designs. Jung, in his writing, spoke of pre-existent pathways in the psyche and I have often thought that labyrinths might be images of those pathways.

If we look at the origins of the word *labyrinth* we discover more of its connection to the Feminine. In one source, it is derived from the root word *labrys*, meaning "double axe." This relates to the many double-axe carvings found by Sir Arthur Evans in his excavations at Knossos on Crete, where the myth of Theseus and Ariadne is purported to have taken place. It is interesting to note that the double-axe motif mounted between bovine horns is among the holiest of symbols in the Minoan Moon-Goddess cult found in Crete, thus further connecting the labyrinth to its Feminine source. *Labrys* also refers to a "place of stone," taking us back to the original caves where labyrinths were found. *Labrys* is also known as "lip," referring to the labia protecting the passage to the womb. Whichever definition we follow, it is clear that they all have a strong connection to the

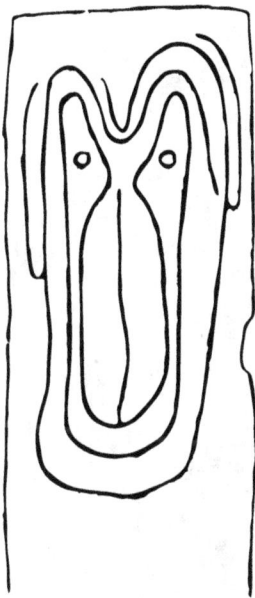

Labyrinth from a passage at Luffang.

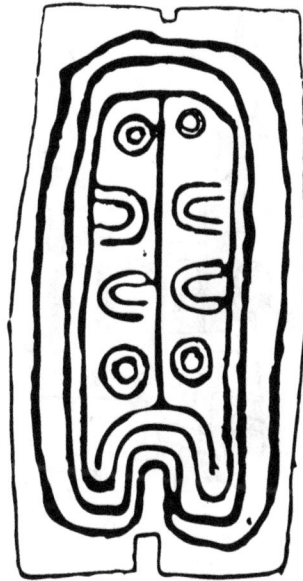

Churinga symbols from Pierres Plates.

Serpent maze from Pierres Plates.

Enclosure at La Pasiega.

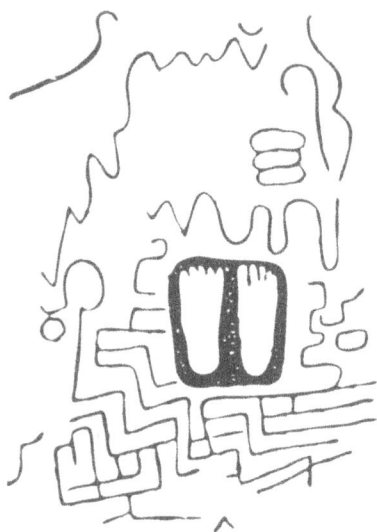

Feet in maze at Petit Mont.

Beak-and-eyebrow motif joined
with oval vulva (c. 3000 B.C.).

Feminine, whether it is the Goddess, the cave as a symbol of the
body of the Great Mother, or the physical body of an actual
woman.

The Archetypal Dimension

What is an archetype? Jung said an image can be considered archetypal when it can be shown to exist in different records of
human history in identical form and with the same meaning. This
is certainly true of the labyrinth. Archetypes can never be fully
known. We can only know them by their symbolic representations
and their images. These separate images combine to give us a
fuller picture of the archetype. Mother is an archetype which we
can know in many ways, for example: our personal mother,
others' mothers, mother as nurturer, mother as destroyer, mother

in the animal kingdom, or the Great Mother. None of these is the whole, but each helps us to understand the whole. The same is true of the symbol of the labyrinth, which is one of the reasons it is so intriguing. It contains within it the numinosity, the mystery, and the multidimensionality of the archetype, with all the promises of possibility that that entails.

Archetypal images serve to take us out of the realm of the mundane and personal, out of the realm of no hope. For in these images other worlds open up to us. Because these images are the language of the Soul, they give us a sense of what is possible. Dreams are our major personal access to this realm. Fairy tales and myths fascinate us for the same reasons. Through working with images, we realize that our deepest fears, our most profound regrets, and our sense of hope or no hope are not ours alone but connect us with those who have come before and will come after.

When we begin to respond to life in its archetypal dimension, we become open to the mystery, to other levels of meaning, to other ways of being, and to synchronous events. The images in your dreams have a personal significance specific to you the dreamer, but they also carry a universal, numinous meaning that takes you out of yourself. It is the interplay between the personal and the archetypal in our dreams—sometimes playful, sometimes painful, sometimes conflictual—that gives them their juice. Opening up a dialogue with the images, moving between the conscious and unconscious, and allowing ourselves to revel in their archetypal perspective liberates us from viewing our lives as limited by our personal history.

An archetypal view is inherently greater and more inclusive than the conscious, literal, fixed, linear, abstract view with which we might identify. The point is to awaken ourselves to a sense of our unrealized possibilities, and to save us from our sense of isolation and meaninglessness, loneliness, confusion, and joylessness. The purpose is to open up our lives to renewal and reshaping. As we proceed we will be playing with the dance between the personal and the archetypal.

The Labyrinth as "Planned Chaos"

Classical labyrinth texts reveal the labyrinth's duality; embodying both superb design and unfathomable chaos, its elaborate complexity causes admiration or alarm, depending on the observer's point of view and sophistication. This dual potentiality is inherent in unicursal and multicursal mazes alike. . . . Yet viewed from above, considered as product rather than process, either design seems admirably intricate and, most likely, highly symmetrical; an image of order containing and controlling magnificent complexity. Both designs are thus planned Chaos.[3]

Most mythological stories of creation begin with form coming out of chaos. Chaos is a state of confusion and disorder. It is a state, psychologically speaking, that we would like to keep at bay. We unconsciously create defensive structures to protect ourselves in the same way that primitive peoples created defensive structures around their holy places. They wanted to keep chaos out and order in. So do we. But, if form has come from chaos, do we not need chaos in order to create new forms? Is chaos not an essential ingredient of the healing process?

In science, chaos is really the study of irregularity. Recent investigations have discovered patterns in what was until now accepted as inevitable disorder. Once scientists could program their computers to scan more data than was previously humanly possible, they were able to discover patterns in what was previously believed to be chaos. If there are patterns in disorder, then is there such a thing as disorder? Could we hypothesize that within every "mess" there is an archetypal structure of order of which we may not be conscious?

To some physicists, the study of chaos is the study of *process* rather than *state,* of becoming rather than of being. It is the science of the nonlinear rather than the linear and by our definition of the Feminine, it is about the Feminine. James Gleick notes, "That twisted changeability (of nonlinear systems) makes nonlinearity hard to calculate, but it also creates rich kinds of behavior

---

3. Penelope Reed Doob, *The Idea of the Labyrinth*, p. 52.

that never occur in linear systems. . . . Analyzing the behavior of a nonlinear equation . . . is like walking through a maze whose walls rearrange themselves with each step you take."[4] Nonlinearity leads to unlimited possibilities. If we compare this to the labyrinth, the process of dancing is what releases the energy for transformation. The Feminine and therefore the labyrinth are about process and nonlinearity.

In chaos theory, if you can visualize the shape, you can understand the system. You must be able to observe the system from a great distance or in huge numbers, both of which were impossible before the advent of computers. The Lorenz Attractor creates a butterfly image very similar in shape to a double spiral/labyrinth and reminds me of the shapes created by Le-Hev-Hev for the Malekula (see Chapter 2 opener). Events may appear to us as chaos in our human lives because we are unable to see the larger pattern into which our particular chaos fits.

> Soon, when scientists saw what computers had to show, it seemed like a face they had been seeing everywhere, in the music of turbulent flows or in clouds scattered like veils across the sky. Nature was constrained. Disorder was channelled, it seemed, into patterns with some common underlying theme.[5]

What happens if we juxtapose the above quote with the following definitions of archetype by Jung?

> Archetypes are, by definition, factors and motifs that arrange the psychic elements into certain images, characterized as archetypal, but in such a way that they can be recognized from the effects they produce.[6]

and

> Psychologically . . . the archetype as an image of instinct is a Spiritual goal toward which the whole nature of man strives; it

---

4. James Gleick, *Chaos—Making a New Science,* p. 24.
5. Gleick, p.152.
6. C. G. Jung, *Collected Works 11,* par. 222.

is the sea to which all rivers wend their way, the prize which the hero wrests from the fight of the dragon.[7]

Have scientists discovered the physical manifestation of a psychic component that Jung intuited so many years ago? Is it possible that the labyrinth patterns, which seem archetypal to me, have also indicated a deeper structure present in the teeming chaos of human existence? Is it possible that as human beings some part of us is attracted to a particular, archetypal labyrinthine energy, and that this energy determines the direction of our lives? When I danced the labyrinth for the first time in New York State, that was the sense I had.

One of the main facets that chaos theory has added to other disciplines is the idea of the position of the observer. Gleick says that as soon as you are involved in the process, you are no longer the objective observer. Not only that, but the position from which you observe has a tremendous influence on what you see.

We can have pictures of labyrinths to hold in our hands and to look at on walls or on floors. In each of those instances, because of the position we take in relation to it, the labyrinth is something different. When I hold a picture in my hand, I am bigger and it is to me a complex and intricate puzzle. When I look at the pattern on the floor, it is bigger than I am but still small enough that I can see the whole pattern. When I am actually dancing the labyrinth and I become absorbed in the turn I am making at the moment, it is easy to lose my way and forget where I am going. Similarly when I am in the labyrinth of my life, I may not know I am in a labyrinth at all. I may not realize that I am on a path and that the path is leading me. I may not feel the powerful magnetic pull of the center that keeps me moving and striving, and yet I follow it. If we go even larger still, perhaps we are attracted to others who are attracted to the same labyrinth we are, and our paths may cross and intertwine. It is endlessly fascinating to conjecture!

7. C. G. Jung, *Collected Works 8*, par. 414.

Walk to the well.
Turn as the earth and the moon turn,
circling what they love.
Whatever circles comes from the center.[8]
 —Rumi

---

8. John Moyne and Coleman Barks, *Unseen Rain: Quatrains of Rumi*, p. 8.

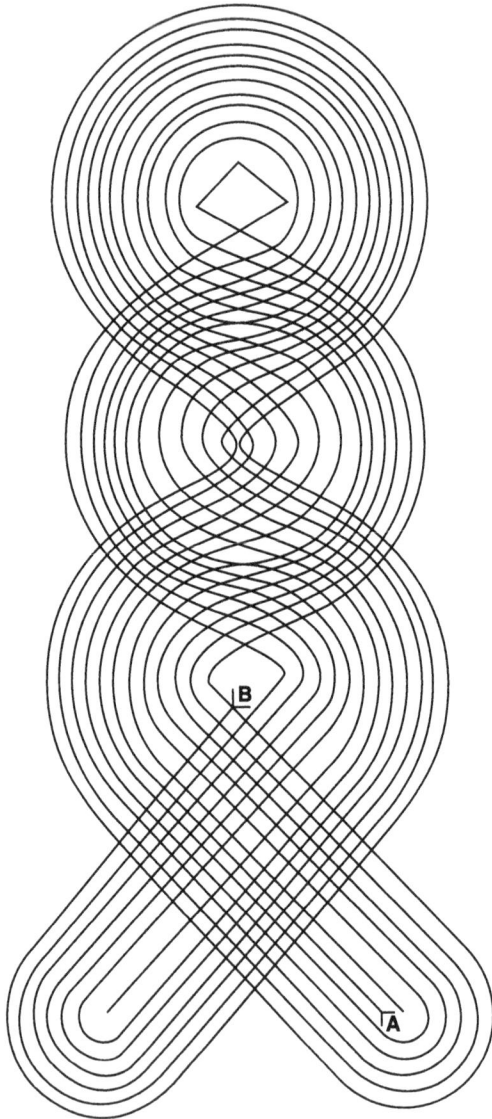

The Malekula labyrinth.

2

THE LABYRINTH
AS SYMBOL

*If the mind makes use of images to grasp the ultimate reality
of things, it is just because reality manifests itself in contra-
dictory ways and therefore cannot be expressed in concepts.
. . . It is therefore the image as such, as a whole bundle of
meanings, that is true and not any one of its meanings, nor
one alone of its frames of reference. To translate an image
into a concrete terminology by restricting it to any one of its
frames of reference is to do worse than mutilate it—it is to
annihilate, to annul it as an instrument of cognition.*[1]

—Mircea Eliade

How is the labyrinth a symbol of the Feminine? First let me clar-
ify what I mean by symbol. Something is symbolic when exploring
its meaning expands our awareness beyond what we already
know. Symbols open doors to potentials that seemed closed before. Symbols are meant to be "played with," and as we do this,

1. Mircea Eliade, *Images and Symbols*, p.15.

endless possibilities unfold. As the quote above states so emphatically, if we restrict our interpretation of a symbol to one thing, we "mutilate it . . . annihilate [and] annul it" as an instrument for our further growth and development.

The labyrinth is a perfect example of a symbol. The more we work with it the more profoundly meaningful it becomes, and our perspectives of it and the world around us keep broadening. I have been working with the labyrinth as a symbol for fourteen years and it is still my teacher.

One thing the labyrinth gives us that other symbols may not is a physical presence with which we can engage. We can walk it, thus involving our whole bodies; we can trace it on a finger labyrinth; we can create ritual in it; and we can be alone or in community as we connect with it. All of these deepen its meaning for us. There are many ways that the labyrinth is a symbol for the Feminine and Soul life journey.

As a Spiritual Container

> Spirit is the centre of life, the light out of which we are born with eyes still reflecting the vastness, and the light toward which our eyes turn when our breath goes out and does not come in again.[2]

Spirit is given, underlies all things, and is always present. It is the matrix of compassion out of which we are born and in which we are held. Connecting to Spirit and allowing ourselves to be penetrated or held in Spirit gives us the story, the foundation, and the basis for understanding reality and the mysteries of existence.

Soul, on the other hand, is about the juiciness of life. It searches for ways to feel alive. It lives with the passions: despair, love, hate, rage, and jealousy. Soul, the lover of beauty, good music, chocolate truffles, and walks in the rain, is held in the bosom of Spirit where it can sing its song, and push the boundaries of the known.

2. John Tarrant, *The Light Inside the Dark*, p.12.

Soul does not abolish the difficulty of our lives, but brings a music to our pains—its gift is to make us less perfect and more whole.[3]

The labyrinth is the perfect symbol of the dance between Soul and Spirit. The container of the labyrinth is present, never changing, holding us as we walk it. Yet we can walk it in myriad ways, pushing its boundaries to learn more about ourselves and growing into who we really are. It is so easy to forget that we live our lives contained within Spirit. Looking at the labyrinth reminds us. Walking into the labyrinth reminds us. When a labyrinth is laid on the ground, it becomes like a lightning rod or a reservoir for spiritual energy to collect.

I have had the privilege of being in various locations on the planet where the energy of Spirit seems to gather. Findhorn in Scotland was one of these places. So was the Jung Institute in Zurich, as was the location where I did my training with Jean Houston. So much attention has been focused on Spirit in these locations that it manifests in abundance. I imagine it saying, "Oh yes, here is a place where I am known, where I can be present and allow magic to happen."

How do we know when Spirit is present? When an inordinate number of synchronistic events occur in one place, and when people mysteriously and magically get what they need when they need it (often in bizarre and strange ways), then Spirit is present.

My favorite personal story of Spirit's appearance also happened to me in the Jean Houston training. After two years of intensity, having my introversion challenged by the extremely extroverted environment of the program, I considered dropping out and not completing the final year. I skipped a class with several friends, and over ice cream sundaes told them of my decision. They said all the appropriate things about how much they would miss me. We returned to the camp. The sessions were held in a huge gymnasium and the washrooms were on a mezzanine looking down over the space. I was in the washroom and heard a drum roll,

3. Tarrant, p.18.

reminding me they were going to draw the ticket for a fund-raising raffle one of the participants had initiated. She wanted to create a training video for parents and had asked for our contributions. I had purchased a ticket.

I left the washroom and could hear that the winner was about to be announced. Leaning against the railing (and I am so thankful the railing was there), I heard my name called. The prize was a year's free tuition for the final year of the program! Other than winning $3 on a lottery ticket, I have never before or since won anything. The message was loud and clear. Spirit had spoken and I felt I had no choice but to listen. I was meant to finish the program. If I had quit, I would not have had the river experience, I probably would not have gone to Zurich, and I would not have written this book.

How does Spirit manifest when the labyrinth is approached with the right intention? I have witnessed incredible things happen for people as they have engaged with it. Often, there is unexpected emotion as people experience themselves being held in loving Feminine energy. We go through much "sacred kleenex" in the workshops. Although I am speaking literally here, the same is true when the labyrinth is experienced symbolically.

One of many examples concerns a woman who was the assistant fire chief of the community where the workshop took place. As you can imagine, she knew the destructive and lethal side of fire only too well. In the workshop, she was exposed to the spiritual and healing aspects of fire and was in a profound dilemma as she struggled to hold the tension of these opposites. During the workshop, people are given an opportunity to create and perform a ritual within the sacred space of the group energy and the container of the labyrinth. Walking very slowly, with deep concentration and holding a piece of paper in her hand, she wound her way to the center. After standing in silence for some time and with great deliberation, she lit the piece of paper in the central flame while at the same time wetting the palm of her other hand in a bowl of water that was there. She placed the burning paper in her wet palm, letting it burn until it got too hot, at which point she transferred it to her other hand. She repeated the ritual until the paper burned up. I was standing beside her and was profoundly moved by the intensity and numinosity of the moment and her effort to hold the opposites of creation and destruction literally in the palm of her hand. With Spirit's presence creating safety and containment, her Soul was given the opportunity to heal a split.

Another example is the following account by a woman who experienced the healing of a childhood wound while standing in the center surrounded by the group.

> Before walking the labyrinth with the group I asked that the fear which is locked in my body be released. Walking to the center is a profoundly stirring experience. In the center a flood of tears rolls down my face. The pain and fear is so great I think I might faint, however, I'm also aware of feeling very safe—carried and contained somehow. I have the following waking dream:
>
> "I'm in a dark bedroom and open the closet door. On the floor a child is crying. She looks up in fear. When she looks at me I suddenly see myself from her eyes—a young woman with black, wild, windswept hair (like a witch)—and on my face is an expression of great love and acceptance. I encourage the child to come out but she's reluctant. I tell her it is safe and gently scoop her up in my arms and lift her out. The closet is full of light. I see pink roses. We step through the doorway into a garden of pink roses. I am standing beside my father who is on my left. He's a younger man wearing jeans and a blue and yellow checked shirt. I say to him, 'It's all right, Dad, I'm not afraid of you anymore.'"

The final example I will give happened on a women's retreat. On this particular occasion the group gathered after dinner when it was already dark outside. The labyrinth took up half the room and we lit the candles on it (one at every turn) as well as placing candles and ritual objects (water, incense, bells) in the center. The group, standing in the other half of the room and facing away from the labyrinth was led in a series of yoga postures called the salutation to the moon (it was also a full moon). We had chanting music softly playing in the background. Drawing the process to its end, Barb Quinlan, the yoga teacher, had us stand with our eyes closed and feel the new energy moving through our bodies. She then suggested we turn around and slowly open our eyes. Perceiving the labyrinth from this altered state of consciousness caused most of us to gasp. Its beauty glowed. It was as if Spirit had descended on the room and enveloped us in her sacredness. Of the hundreds of times I have walked the labyrinth this was the most profound.

Because I work as an analyst, I am very aware that the same kind of spiritual energy can also be present in the analytical container. When a sacred space is created in the room where the analysis takes place, it is like crossing the threshold into the labyrinth. A healing field emerges that holds and guides the process. It is the energy of Spirit containing Soul.

As the Rhythm of Soul and Life

If we look at the labyrinth again, we can see that the twists and turns constituting its body are the pathways of Soul, of the Feminine. They mirror for us the flow of psychic energy as Jung described it. There is a continuous movement forward (progression), which is always followed by a movement backward (regression), which is always followed by a movement forward, and so on. This is the movement of life. It is the flow between any two opposites, whether between darkness and light, introversion and extroversion, or joy and sorrow.

This message is important to explore in our world of today where we have lost touch with what it means to live in the mystery of existence. Most of us get caught up in the ebb and flow of daily life, following paths laid out for us by social structures we have come to accept as the norm. We forget that life is not lived in a straight line. We forget that death is always sitting on our left shoulder. We forget that disintegration and decay are the truth for all life forms on this planet.

How often do we rail at God because of the losses we have had to experience, the illnesses that have plagued us, the pain we have

suffered? If we do not blame God or some unknown universal
force, we blame ourselves. It is my fault. I am a terrible human
being. I am guilty of so much, this must be my punishment or my
karma. Maybe. Maybe some of those things are true to some degree. But, the more universal truth is that *life is like that*. That is
the way of the Feminine. Life follows the rhythm of progression
and regression, forward and backward movement, birth and
death, creation and destruction. That is one of the profound messages being communicated to us by the labyrinth. Our ancestors
knew this truth and we are being given the opportunity to learn
it too.

Walking the labyrinth with our physical bodies allows us to
learn this message in a way that bypasses the mind and penetrates
the nervous system. Our bodies begin to learn this forward and
backward rhythm and we begin to accept it on a level of body and
nervous system—a level of knowing that gets imbued in our cells
and not just our intellect.

As Goddess of the Moon

The Goddess of Paleolithic times was the Goddess of the Moon.
During the process of writing this book, I went on retreat in the
Santa Cruz mountains in California. I began the retreat during a
full moon whose light filled the night and, for me, made it feel as
safe as day. As the moon began to wane, it came up later and later.
Being away from any lights of civilization, the darkness was profound. It carried the mystery of the unseen and made me aware of
my own fears of what might be lurking there. I left on the night
when there was no moon. In fact the darkness of the moon lasted
for three days. This experience reawakened my awareness of how
important the light of the moon must have been and how she was
missed when she was not present. Her cyclical nature was a powerful teacher and marker of time. The importance of the cycles of
no moon, waxing moon, full moon, and waning moon spawned
many rituals of worship that are honored today by full-moon
meditation ceremonies.

Walking the labyrinth follows these four phases of the moon. We can experience it from two perspectives. In the first instance, before we enter the labyrinth, we are in the dark. As we spiral inward we embody the waxing phase. Once we are in the center, it is like being blessed with the light, power, and energy of the full moon. Our movement back out is the waning moon, until we again reach the place of darkness, stillness, or no movement.

Or, from the second perspective we can see the center as the place of death and rebirth found in the inner recesses of the cave where it was very dark. We can view the journey as its opposite. Before we enter, we are in light but spurred to this journey so our light can be even brighter. We move away from the brightness as the moon wanes and find ourselves in the stillness and darkness of the center, staying as long as is needed until we move slowly into rebirth. The moon waxes and we find that when we have exited and integrated our learning, the light is brighter than ever.

As the Way

In the discussion of chaos, I hypothesized that the labyrinth is a map of our journey in life. When we are walking it, we live in the moment, one step at a time, interacting with what is in front of us on the path. By looking at the pattern as a whole, we get an overview and a sense that we are indeed living in a larger story, and that there is some order in what feels like chaos.

The way, the path, the journey, or the dance to the center is a difficult one, filled with obstacles and challenges. In my work as an analyst and in the personal journey of my own life, it has been crucial for me to know that there was some order to the chaos I was experiencing, some sense to my suffering, some path that I was following. A picture of the labyrinth on the wall of my consulting room has become that symbol for me and the work with my analysands.

The idea of walking in archetypal, ancient pathways fascinates me. Jung spoke about "pre-existent pathways" that we have inherited from our ancestors. "The mind, as the active principle in the inheritance, consists of the sum of the ancestral minds, the 'unseen fathers' whose authority is born anew in the child."[4]

As we continue to dance the labyrinth of our lives, we can draw up into consciousness deeper and deeper levels of the archetypal substrata on which we exist. The deeper we go, the more evident it becomes that we are indeed the inheritors and carriers of a deep ancestral mind of both the "unseen fathers" and "unseen mothers." Knowing that this dance is our life, the more often we respond to the call of the numinous center—the Self, with a sense of being and devotion, the more we will know these ancient pathways within us.

As Ancestral Line

In the quotation above I believe Jung is referring to the genetic ancestral line from which we have come. Evidence shows that in our biology we also carry the cellular, emotional, and historical story of the line of people from whom we have physically descended. We have a certain way of being in the world, a temperament, a taste for certain foods, an affinity for places, music, and so on. We also carry inside of us attitudes, emotional patterns, and stories. We live from these stories in a way many of us are not aware of. These stories inform our nervous systems. Memories of those who have genetically come before us have been stored on a cellular level. Some of the unconscious scripts we carry come from that level of ourselves.

For women who are trying to forge new paths, the unconscious messages can be things such as, "Women in our family don't do that"; "Women in our family would never defy the natural order of things"; and, "If you dare to move beyond the strictures we have accepted for centuries, you will be betraying a sacred trust you have with us." "We have chosen the path of safety. We want you to be safe. We might have been very unhappy but at least we were safe"; "We knew our place in the world. What are you doing

4. C. G. Jung, *Collected Works 8,* par. 97–98.

risking what has been true for so long?"; "Look at those who risked and dared in the past. They were burned as witches. That will happen to you too. Be safe. Be careful. Hide."

Most often we are not conscious of these hidden voices, we just know that we feel terror at stepping out into the world, horrific anxiety at showing who we really are, anguish that maybe we don't have the knowledge or the strength or the guts to carry this off. It is all too hard. Mainly we are confused. What is the story we want to write with our lives? Is it the old one of safety or the new one of risk and adventure?

What gives hope, makes life interesting, and leads to change is the other part of the story. What if Jung is not referring to our ancestral genetic line? What if he is referring to our "Soul Line"? What do I mean by "Soul Line"? Most world religions, in either their traditional or mystical paths, have a theory of reincarnation. Usually it is proposed that some part of us does not die (the Soul) and that each time we return we are challenged to grow and develop in different ways, sometimes repairing what may have gone wrong in a previous lifetime (karma). People can be referred to as "old Souls." Perhaps you have encountered very young children who give the impression of having great wisdom. It is also proposed that before we incarnate we choose the family we will come into for the learning it will give us in terms of the development of our Souls.

Maybe Jung was actually referring to both. Maybe he is referring to a *conjunctio* (sacred joining) of the ancestral genetic line and the ancestral Soul line. Let's imagine that this is true. If so, then with each birth we have a marriage of the cellular/genetic story with Soul/Spirit story. This hypothesis is a way to understand some of the complexity and mystery of our human existence. Because the labyrinth is a physical presence that we walk, we can imagine it holds symbolically the cellular genetic story we have been born into. When we enter the labyrinth we bring with us our soul story. As we walk the labyrinth our soul story intermingles with our genetic cellular story and a new story is created. I will return to this theme later in the book.

As Temenos, Container, and Alchemical Vessel

A temenos is a sacred space. A space is sacred because it contains a certain numinosity and is separated off from the profane world around it. We step over the threshold into sacred space and sacred time. It is here that communion with the gods is possible. When the sacred manifests itself in space, the real unveils itself and the world comes into existence. We have already discussed how the labyrinth creates sacred space.

Jung speaks at length of the alchemical vessel and the Opus, or life work of the alchemist. The alchemists were dealing with physical matter (chemistry), the mysteries of the universe (Spirit), and the interrelationship of themselves with both. Within the contained space of the labyrinth, all the elements of who we are on a physical, psychological, mythic, and spiritual level have a chance to interact. Because the labyrinth is a container wherein movement can occur, it provides us with a boundary we can bump up against. This boundary creates a certain amount of tension, which produces the heat that stimulates transformation, just as fire catalyzes the alchemical transformation of base products into gold.

As Initiation Process

> It is probable that the very word *initiation* in English comes from the Latin word *inire*, enter, to signify ritual entry into the earth.[5]

By entering into the labyrinth we are invited to participate in a process of initiation, just as entry into the underworld signifies an opportunity for death and rebirth. Eliade says this type of initiation occurs in connection with a mystical vocation. The initiate chooses either to voluntarily participate or he or she is *called* to do so. "The initiation process is a fundamental existential

---

5. Jackson Knight, *Cumean Gates*, p. 45.

experience because through it a man (woman) becomes able to assume his (her) mode of being in its entirety."[6]

There are three phases to the basic initiation pattern. These include a rite of separation, which leads to a rite of transition, and ends with a rite of incorporation. If we look at the temenos of the labyrinth, the separation between profane and sacred space occurs at the entry. It is an acknowledgment of, and a commitment to, a journey of inner exploration. Transitional space is in the labyrinthine character of forward and backward movement, as well as the entry into the center. The center, where both the gods and demons live, is where incorporation takes place. After transformation, the labyrinth gives us the opportunity to follow its pathways from the center back to the outside.

Initiation is the archetypal pattern by which the psyche, whether in individuals or in groups of people, is enabled to make a transition from one stage of development to another and, therefore, brings the theme of death and rebirth into focus. "For what initiation does is irrevocably alter where knowledge is centred."[7]

As Body of the Great Mother

While leading labyrinth workshops, I generally give the participants an opportunity to first walk the labyrinth as a group. We do this by holding hands and entering the sacred space. Often, the winding in and out requires us to move between two rows of people and it feels as if we are being squeezed through the birth canal. At the center, we spiral together into the space and with close body contact become one breathing, swaying organism. Often, participants are moved to tears as we stay in this safe and womb-like container sometimes for fifteen minutes. It is difficult to pull myself away as I lead the group back out again. Each time I feel the separation of birth, and others comment on this as well.

Just as the womb is a boundary within which the growing child can move and grow until it is ready to be born into another stage

---

6. Eliade, *Rites and Symbols of Initiation*, p. 3.
7. Vivian Darroch-Lozowski, "Initiation in Hermeneutics," p. 243.

of being, so the labyrinth, representating the womb of the Great Mother, offers us a contained space to re-experience the movement and struggle that growth, birth, and rebirth entail.

As Organs of the Body

Following upon the theme of the Great Mother is the organicity of the labyrinth itself. We find it in the movement and shape of the labyrinth that echoes parts of the human body. The ancient Assyrians used the entrails of sacrificial animals for prophecy.

My first degree was in occupational therapy. Included in our training was the awesome experience of dissecting human cadavers. I remember my astonishment at the length and convoluted, labyrinthine state of the intestines. You can see in the diagrams here the similarity between the convolutions in the brain and its structure and the structure of the labyrinth. We also know of the labyrinth in the inner ear—an appropriate place for a labyrinth since we often refer to intuition as inner hearing.

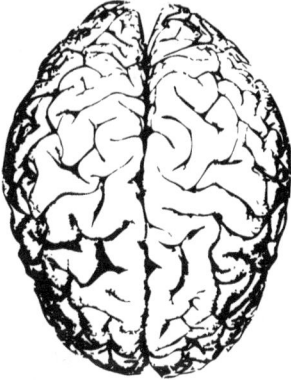

There is a resonance between what is physically inside of us and what is outside. Unconsciously, we know this when we walk the labyrinth. This is one of the reasons why the labyrinth is becoming such an important healing tool. The forward and backward movement stimulates the neurons in our brains to cross over the midline; therefore,

uniting both sides of the brain. This is part of the reason why physically and emotionally we feel so much calmer after we have walked the labyrinth.

As the Center, the Mandala

If the center draws us, what resides there? Because it is a place of stillness, it is where Soul and Spirit can meet and be one. In this place we are at the core of our being, both psychologically and spiritually. The place I reached in the river experience is that place. It is the place reached in the analytical process when all defenses disintegrate and we touch the gold of our being. Sometimes Spirit and light are more prevalent and we find ourselves held in bliss. Sometimes the dark is more prevalent, and we face parts of ourselves that have been hidden, unknown, and rejected.

Images for what we encounter in the center come to us from mythology. In the myth of Theseus and the Minotaur, Theseus, holding Ariadne's thread, meets the Minotaur (a monster that is half man, half bull, and his half brother). The Minotaur, who subsists on human flesh, is symbolic of the devouring nature of our unresolved complexes. In the myth of her descent to the underworld, Inanna, the Sumerian Queen of Heaven, meets Erishkigal, her dark sister, who is dirty and naked, alone and lonely, full of pain and rage. These stories will be dealt with in more depth in Chapters 6 and 8.

The individuation process, becoming fully who we are, is also the story of the integration of the dark and the light. It begins with our birth and ends with our death. It is the story of how we integrate Soul and Spirit and are guided by the Self (with a capital S). Our belief systems are the stories we tell ourselves about who we are and the world we live in. These stories give us an orientation in the world, whether they move us toward the light or give us an experience of the dark.

"The goal is neither height nor depth but the centre," Jung said.[8] The center of the labyrinth is the place where the energies of

8. C. G. Jung, *Collected Works 13*, par. 333.

the heavenly Spirit world above meet the chaotic underworld below. Eliade traces this idea back to the Babylonians and the early Hebrews.[9] In Babylon, there was the Gate of Apsu; *apsu,* meaning the waters of chaos before the Creation. Among the Hebrews we find the Rock of Jerusalem, which went deep down into the subterranean waters of *Tehom* or Chaos. There was, likewise, a gate to the gods above, through which they came down to earth. It reminds me of the Hopi tradition of humankind being fashioned at the navel of the earth. We end at the same place we began.

The cosmic tree is a perfect symbol for this central place, for it occupies three planes of existence. Its roots go deep into the earth, its branches reach upward toward the heavens, and its trunk makes its presence felt very strongly on the human plane. The shamanic journey takes place in this central place, the initiation of the shaman consisting of his or her ability to freely move up and down the tree to access all realms.

The center is by far the most powerful place in the labyrinth. It is Home. It is where we come to rest, the place of peace and transformation. It is also the place of chaos and turmoil, where all movement has stopped and there is time to absorb. It is the place of the whirlwind—it is all movement. The intersection of vertical and horizontal planes and their concomitant energies is the strongest here. It is where the gods, both in their dark and light aspects, come to meet us. It is the goal and the origin. We both begin and end here—birth and death—the place of paradox.

As Fortress

In prehistoric times the labyrinth was used to protect the gods and goddesses in the center from the evils (other gods and goddesses) that may be found outside. Ancient tombs built on the labyrinthine pattern protected the treasures and body of the king from thieves, but also allowed only those who had the right of entry to go in. Labyrinthine walls have been built around cities

9. Eliade, *Images*, p. 53.

such as Troy as protection from enemies, and strategic war maneuvers used these same principles.

> The very enactment by moving on a labyrinthine path may be expected to exercise a labyrinthine, exclusive effect. That is the meaning of a maze dance or other maze ritual. The movements of the performers are intended to weave a magical entanglement and spread a field of magical force to exclude all that is not wanted to enter the guarded place.[10]

As Dance

Theseus and his friends were purported to have performed the Crane Dance on the island of Delos in celebration of their escape from the Cretan labyrinth. The dance was thought to have received its name either because the movements of the dancers resembled the bird in flight or because their costumes looked like cranes. No one knows for sure. Dances of similar character were mentioned by both Homer in the *Iliad* and Virgil in the *Aeneid*. There is also some thought that these were ceremonial dances associated with the awakening of nature in spring.

The fact that the labyrinth is "danced" adds the important dimension of embodiment. I use *danced* interchangeably with *walked* because it conveys a sense of fluid movement because the experience is one of integration of the body and the mind that has the power to transform. The labyrinth dance unites life and death by moving backward and forward in both directions. Labyrinthine dances still survive on Crete.

As Movement of the Snake

Most of us are both fascinated and repulsed by snakes. Archetypally, the snake holds many levels of meaning. Those of us raised in a Judeo-Christian environment have had to deal with the snake as a symbol of evil. If we trace the history of those beliefs backward

10. Knight, p. 76.

in time, it becomes clear that the snake was a powerful "familiar" of the Great Goddess. The snake, a creature living in the bowels of the earth, carried the wisdom of cold, ruthless instinctuality, while at the same time symbolizing rebirth by shedding its skin. Patriarchal monotheism needed to depotentiate the Goddess by attempting to devalue Her knowing, in order to have society value the light of consciousness and the invisible God. Separating from the sacrality of the dark and moving into the sacrality of the light was part of our spiritual evolution as a species. If the snake symbolizes Feminine wisdom, our attitude toward snakes often mirrors our attitude to those dark, feminine aspects of ourselves. We are fortunate to be living in a time where for some of us these two worlds are, though with some pain, beginning to integrate. The labyrinth journey is a place where that can begin to happen.

Here is a dream of a fifty-year-old woman as she begins to connect with the power of the Feminine within herself.

> I dreamed of snakes, all intertwined, moving along with a single purpose . . . all moving, undulating in one direction. It gave me quite a start. I headed uphill to a barn to safety. Once inside, I realized it was empty—deserted. I looked over to my left and saw about 20 feet away an immense cobra. Its head was a foot long, at least, and it was perhaps two feet thick and 13 or 14 feet long. We were both perfectly still. At first I felt afraid, but then realized it was a sign of something. I felt a tremendous respect for its power and started to back slowly out of the barn. When I recognized what it was, it lifted its head and looked directly at me.

We can see that her initial fear of the cobra turns into recognition and respect once she acknowledges its power. At that moment the cobra lifts its head and in turn acknowledges her. The opportunity for relationship has been established.

As mentioned earlier, when I walk the labyrinth with a group of people we often begin by holding hands and creating one large, imaginary snake. We follow the twists and turns of the labyrinth as a snake follows the twists and turns of the earth. It is a powerful experience to be a part of such a moving, sinuous organism that coils into itself in the center. We stay there for a while, breathing and rocking as one, experiencing what it is like to be together, held in the womb of Earth, Goddess, or Universe until we are ready to uncoil and wind our way back out again.

As Altered State of Consciousness

Vincent Scully, in his architectural descriptions of ancient Greece, refers over and over again to the labyrinthine way found in most temples. He cites Knossos, Samos, Eleusis, Epidaurus, Ephesos, Ptoon, Delphi, Samothrace, and the Acropolis. These "ways" sometimes led up from the sea or down into a valley. They would lead the people on a long, circuitous journey, sometimes entering buildings, going from light to darkness to light. There was a purpose in these snakelike approaches and it was to prepare people for what they might meet at the place of power—the center of the ritual. People's state of consciousness needed to be altered, leaving the profane world outside and preparing themselves for the sacred world within.

The path of the labyrinth is long because we are being prepared for the sacred center, and by the time we reach it, our consciousness is indeed altered. Having to return over the same path in order to exit the labyrinth gives us the opportunity to integrate what has occurred in the center, and again our consciousness is altered.

As Choice

Because the unicursal labyrinth has only one path, we might think choice has been eliminated. This is not so. It is filled with an infinite number of choices that mirror the ones we make minute-by-minute in our everyday lives. The most important choice we make is whether to begin or not. If the call is strong enough it might feel as if there is no choice, for a refusal can result in illness or misfortune. Perhaps it becomes a dance of the Ego (that part of us that wants things its way and might feel quite lazy) struggling against or interacting with the pull of the Self (the Divine part of ourselves) that calls us on our larger journey.

Let's play with the idea of physically dancing the labyrinth. You can imagine the many possibilities for moving through it. One can vary the pace; one can walk, crawl, kneel, sit, ride, push, or pull one's way through. One can face forward or backward, move steadily or haltingly, be focused or unfocused, have a deep purpose or seek a purpose, be blind or wide-eyed. Like life and the way we live our lives, the possibilities are too numerous to count. When dancing the labyrinth with other people, it's fascinating to notice who you pass and who passes you. We all seem to be moving on the same predetermined pathway, and yet find ourselves in very different positions at different times. Some people are in your rhythm and time frame and seem to move along with you, while others don't meet you at all. All of this can change in an instant as you or someone else makes a choice to alter what is being done.

As a Game

Karl Kerenyi, the noted Hungarian mythologist who was a friend of Jung's, speaks of "labyrinthine joy." What a wonderful expression! He describes it as being pagan and secular as opposed to Christian and penitent. The labyrinth at Chartres is covered with chairs most of the time. I have wondered if one of the reasons is the management's wish to discourage the playful, childlike attitude that dancing the labyrinth can bring to those who participate.

In recent years awareness of both the Divine Child and the personal inner child and their place in our lives has grown. If we could approach life with the wonder and astonishment of the child, how much more could we bring to life and life bring to us? Joy, laughter, humor, a sense of fun and the ridiculous, a sense of the mysterious, the sacred, and the possible are invaluable tools as we dance our way through our lives.

People often ask me why this simple circle on the floor should have so much power. Throughout this section I have been exploring the answer to that question. We have looked at the many symbolic meanings of the labyrinth with reference to the spiritual journey it describes and in particular its connection to the Feminine. C. N. Deedes summarizes the mystery, power, and far-reaching impact of the labyrinth as follows:

> Such facts as are known about the labyrinth reveal much of great interest; but the mystery which surrounds it is by no means dispelled. . . . There the king-gods performed magical acts and spoke magical words for the welfare of their people; and the psychological state created thereby in their subjects doubtless produced certain material results. Such conditions are difficult for us now to realize. . . . Above all the labyrinth was the centre of activities concerned with those greatest of mysteries, Life and Death. There men tried by every means known to them to overcome death and to renew life. The labyrinth protected and concealed the dead king-god in order that his life in the afterworld might be preserved. There the living king-god went to renew and strengthen his own vitality by association with the immortal lives of his dead ancestors. The labyrinth was the centre of the strongest emotions of the people—joy, fear and grief were there given the most intense forms of expression. These emotions were directed into certain channels, producing ritual and the earliest forms of art—not only music and dancing but also sculpture and painting. The labyrinth as tomb and temple fostered the development of all art and literature, activities which in those days possessed a religious and life-giving significance.[11]

11. C. N. Deedes, "The Labyrinth," p. 42.

Author's photo of Chartres.

3

THE LABYRINTH
AT CHARTRES

I haven't lived my life chronologically. No one does. Each moment reaches backward and forward to all other moments. The story in the book is the story of my life, but sometimes I've found the image of a later event in an early photograph, and once or twice a late picture was made in the grip of a lost emotion.[1]

—Richard Avendon

The train from Paris to Chartres is the regular commuter train, not too old, not too new, filled with laughing card-playing students, businesspeople, novel-reading or newspaper-reading silent passengers, and parcel-laden shoppers. In amongst this mélange are several who don't quite seem to belong. Their eyes are peeled on the ever-changing countryside. Sometimes they talk to each other, but they are obviously preoccupied, anticipating something.

1. Richard Avendon in *An Autobiography*, NY and London: Random House and Jonathan Cape, 1993.

These are the pilgrims to Chartres, drawn there by the great cathedral built on a mound and the labyrinthine town with the meandering river that surrounds it. But these particular pilgrims have been attracted not only by the awesome architecture, the magnificent stained-glass windows, the intricate carvings, the flying buttresses, the heaven-reaching spires, the long Christian history, but moreso by the ancient labyrinth found laid in stone on the floor of the cathedral.

I made my first pilgrimage to Chartres with great anticipation, only to discover, as so many before me and since have discovered, that the labyrinth is indeed covered with chairs. Only the middle is accessible as you proceed down the aisle to the back of the cathedral. Disappointed as I was, it was awesome to be in the ambience of this incredible Gothic structure. We were told that only on the summer solstice (June 21st) would the chairs be removed. (If you are planning on traveling to Chartres, I suggest you check with the cathedral to see when the labyrinth is cleared for walking.) Thus the seeds were planted for my second pilgrimage and I decided to return on that date.

Arriving at the cathedral early that day, we found many there before us. An interesting phenomenon was in process. People were politely following each other around, and yet there was a huge gap between one group and the next. Leading the second group was a young woman so immersed in her spiritual experience that after each step she would wait several minutes as she communed, while at the same time being totally unaware of the hundreds of people waiting in line behind her to also experience the labyrinth. Unable to tolerate the situation, I left, only to return much later in the afternoon. We had been told that at 5:00 P.M. they would begin putting the chairs back on the labyrinth. It was now 4:30.

I was able to walk the labyrinth and was in a line of six waiting to get into the center. The process adopted here was to allow each individual time alone in the center. The energy generated by the group walking was incredible. The chandelier above the labyrinth was swinging in wide circles even though there were no doors open and no breeze in the room. Two French women before me and I began to chat. All three of us were aware of a heaviness in the air, and in my broken French and their broken English we agreed that the Feminine was missing, nor was there any humor. We decided we would go into the center together and dance the cancan, and that is what we did. What a powerful experience it was to bring life back into the room and to honor the flower of Aphrodite in the center. True to form, as we danced, staff began to put the chairs back on the labyrinth.

The sense you get of Chartres Cathedral's history depends upon whose book you read. Some, such as author Malcolm Miller, an Englishman who has devoted his life to studying the cathedral and to living in the town of Chartres, are very pragmatic, focusing on known details in their historical and aesthetic accounts. The Christians first appear in Chartres around the fourth century, following the Druids. The cathedral was built and burnt down numerous times, the last fire taking place on June 10, 1194. The present building was constructed from 1194 to 1260 at a speed unheard of in that day. This accounts for its architectural homogeneity.[2]

Another perspective is more free-flowing and visionary:

> During the early phase of the Gothic style, bands of faithful enthusiasts—ordinary lay folk under the guidance of architects or assisted by craftsmen—could be found trekking from site to site, carting the bricks and mortar to build another cathedral in honour of the Holy Virgin or God. Many of the cathedrals of northern France were built by this spontaneous lay movement, the "Gothic crusade." They were built in a great wave of mystic fervour, by young people or grown women and men, who were passing the bricks from hand to hand and chanting hymns to the rhythm of their labour, or intoning the holy songs around their campfires at night.

What a wonderful image to hold the energy that went into building the cathedral. The writer goes on:

---

2. Malcolm Miller, *Chartres Cathedral*, p.10.

Nor were professional architects or craftsmen aloof from such impassioned motivations. The truth is, the Gothic cathedral embodies an utterly irrational experiment. The scrupulous know-how that binds the tender filigree of stone with solid physical laws represents a rare union between mystical vision and practical experience. The cathedrals are works of art inspired by visions, not mere buildings, but they are artistic creations in which the technological accomplishment was of the highest degree. Nevertheless, the vision was always the decisive factor.[3]

One of the most important guilds and schools of "artisan-mystics," who came to call themselves Freemasons, was at Chartres Cathedral. "They combined religious and philosophical speculations with the more prosaic rules of construction."[4] Although these people were deemed to be pagan by the church, they were tolerated because of their great skills. Their inner teaching remained a mystery only revealed to their followers as they progressed from grade to grade. Freemasonry developed the mind, educating more and more people to be "freethinkers," something unheard of in the Europe of that time.

This mystery, perhaps extending as far back as the Egyptian pyramids, is imbedded in the sacred architecture of the cathedral and particularly in the sacred geometry of the labyrinth itself.

Louis Charpentier, in his book *The Mysteries of Chartres Cathedral,* weaves a convincing story that begins with the worship of the Goddess in her Celtic roots at this site, and names it as one of the places on our planet that emit high levels of magnetic energy that has drawn worshipers for millennia. He builds a case that the underground wellspring beneath the cathedral was originally a Goddess-worship location and that the original Black Madonna found at Chartres and taken over by the early Christians was, in actuality, a statue of the Goddess placed close to the throbbing energies of Mother Earth.

---

3. Willis Harman, *Higher Creativity,* p.168–69, in a quote from M. Sworder, *Fulcanelli: Master Alchemist—Le Mystere des Cathedrales.*
4. Harman, p. 171.

The labyrinth route.

The Labyrinth

Let's look at the labyrinth in its two-dimensional format. On first glance, one can see that it consists of a series of twists and turns around a still point which is at the center. It appears balanced and symmetrical, but not quite. It is divided into four sections but there are connections between each of the sections, none reaching further than its neighboring quadrant. The center is a circle enclosing the six-petaled flower of Aphrodite.

Like Jung's system of psychic energy, the labyrinth is not a closed system, for there is a way of getting into it both from the outside and from the inside. It follows the progression and regression of the flow of psychic energy. There is a movement forward (progression) balanced by a movement backward (regression).

If you follow the twists and turns beginning at the outside of the circle you will soon realize that you are required to traverse all the twists and turns closest to the center, going through all four quadrants, before you take the turnings near the outside of the circle, again going though all four quadrants. You are then led from there directly into the center of the labyrinth.

Closer inspection shows that whether you enter the labyrinth from the center or from the outside, you enter on the middle or fourth turning of a quadrant in each case. The place of change, where you move from either the inside to the outside turnings or vice-versa (where the diagram changes from broken to solid line), also happens in the fourth or middle turning of the other two quadrants. Just before you enter the final fourth turning that leads you into the center of the labyrinth you are also almost next to the exact spot where you first entered. Just as you near your goal you feel the furthest away.

Within each quadrant, there are seven turns balancing between the left and right directions. When you physically dance or walk it, you become aware that with each turn the focus of your gaze is alternately directed to the inside and to the outside of the labyrinth.

Conty points out the intersection of the axes as they move through the center creates a cross.

> As we follow the transformation step by step, we realize also that the new twist is what produces the central cross— presented by the wall of the labyrinth. We thus obtain a geometric explanation for a more hidden second meaning of the Cross. Besides being a symbol of the meeting of different planes, the image also becomes the symbol of a crossing over or of a rite of passage or even of metanoia: a turn which can reorient and restore the twisted or topsy-turvy psyche of a pilgrim aspiring to transformation on his way in the labyrinth.[5]

5. Patrick Conty, "The Geometry of the Labyinth," p.13.

The Center: Aphrodite's Flower

This particular center is not just a circle but consists of a six-petaled blossom called the flower of Aphrodite. What is Aphrodite's flower doing in this Christian cathedral? According to Barbara Walker, six as a number has Feminine and divine sexual connotations. Christians called it the number of sin, whereas the Pythagoreans called it the perfect number or the Mother.[6]

How powerful to have a symbol for the Divine Feminine, the Goddess, as the grounding center of this experience. Johnson's beautiful description of Aphrodite helps us to understand the divine power of the Feminine as Goddess of love, birth, and death, and how the journey to the center of the labyrinth is our journey to reconnect with her.

> Worship of Aphrodite as the Black Virgin extends from ancient pagan goddess worship to relatively modern times. . . . The promises of love and new life held out by Aphrodite are profound. They go deep into the psyche and change our lives utterly. Love both heals and excites. When we are loved, the world feels refreshed and new; our eyes, both the outer eye and the inner eye, are opened. A radiance transfuses the landscape of our life, changing it completely, overturning everything, shifting our condition, as physical caresses transform our bodies and alter our perceptions. Joy is only the beginning of Aphrodite's heady covenant. It is transformed making us feel reborn even as we are struck with wonder and, perhaps, fear.[7]

Numbers

The numbers four and seven are particularly relevant to the symbolism of the Chartres labyrinth. Four is perhaps the first to catch our eye, as the labyrinth is divided into four quadrants. As we

6. Barbara Walker, *The Woman's Dictionary of Symbols and Sacred Objects*, p. 68.
7. Buffie Johnson, *Lady of the Beasts*, p. 88.

begin to trace the pattern we see that we do not completely cover one quadrant and then go directly to another, but instead begin in one, move on to the next, back to the original, and then on to a third. It is like picking up bits and pieces of story or information along the way and building on them to create a final whole. This is the Feminine way. The process of analysis can seem frustrating unless we trust that each topic explored is a part of the whole, and that each seeming diversion is important. As an analyst, holding the image of the labyrinth in mind helps me hold my center and allow the process of the analysand to unfold.

To Jung, the number four symbolized wholeness, and certainly if we walk all four quadrants we do reach a kind of wholeness. We could also play around with the number four in this perspective. It could represent the four seasons (spring, summer, winter, and fall), or the four elements (water, fire, earth, and air), or the four directions (east, south, west, and north), or the four functions of consciousness according to Jungian typology (thinking, feeling, intuition, and sensation). In each case, passing through the four gives the sense of wholeness for we then come to know each of the elements.

The number seven is also important. In each quadrant there are seven turnings. Again, seven symbolically has many meanings: a number of holiness, completion, creation, purification, initiation, and wisdom. Seven is the number most commonly associated with initiation. It denotes the steps or stages of an inner, as opposed to an outer, journey. Certainly it is a familiar number in the Bible with the seven sacraments and the seven deadly sins. It is often after seven years that debts are forgiven, and we have seven days in the week. According to Hindu tradition there are seven chakras (energy centers) in the body.

The chakras are important for they amplify and deepen the idea of the labyrinth as a process of embodiment. The seven chakras have associated meanings: 7. Crown (Spirituality); 6. Forehead: Intuition; 5. Throat: Expression; 4. Heart: Love; 3. Solar Plexus: Power and Emotion; 2. Sacral: Sexuality and Creativity; 1. Base: Survival and Safety.

Earlier, I mentioned that whether we enter the labyrinth from the inside or the outside, we begin on the fourth turn. The place of change from movement around the center to movement closer to the outside also happens at the fourth turn. We can see here that the fourth chakra involves the heart and love. Nothing can happen without the strong presence of love in our lives on both a personal and spiritual level.

One can play with endless possibilities when looking at the structure of the labyrinth and its elements. Using the chakra metaphor can explain why we traverse the turns closest to the center of the labyrinth first, when we enter from the outside and closest to the outside, or when we enter from the inside. If we number the turns from the inside out, we have the lower numbers near the center and the higher numbers near the outside. In the chakra system, lower numbers have to do with bodily safety and grounding, whereas higher numbers correspond to higher centers of a more spiritual nature.

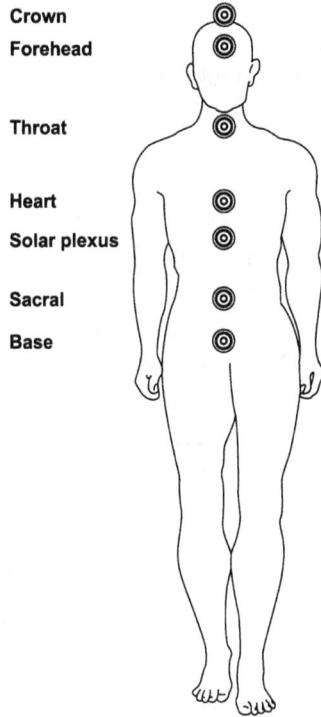

Crown
Forehead
Throat
Heart
Solar plexus
Sacral
Base

The seven major chakras.

When we begin from the center and come from the Self, then spiritual numbers are closer and more familiar to us. We need to become grounded in the lower centers before we emerge into the outside world. The converse is also true. If we come from the outside, we need to make sure of being grounded before we can take in the higher energies that prepare us for entering the rarefied atmosphere of the center.

I invite you to add your speculations to mine, for it helps to make the labyrinth come alive for you personally.

The Ritual

Eliade's words about odyssey (below) bring us back to the theme of this book. We need to embrace all aspects of life, symbolized for us in the image of the dark Feminine. As humans we are a strange lot. We run from pain and sorrow (understandably), but on the other hand, when things are going well we are just as terrified to embrace joy. We crave happiness but feel we don't deserve it. We interpret the coming of bad times as a justifiable punishment for some unknown human flaw. What the labyrinth teaches us, and I cannot emphasize this enough, is that life is about rhythm and flow, times of joy and times of sorrow, times of moving forward, times of moving backward, and times of standing still. These are the archetypal dimensions of the larger pattern, of the larger story, of the mystery of life.

Because of the complexity of the Chartres labyrinth in particular, it becomes a profound tool for internalizing this lesson. We have seen multidimensionality woven together in an elegant, mythical way. It affects us physically, psychologically, emotionally, intellectually, and spiritually. What a gift we have been given!

> Every exile is a Ulysses travelling toward Ithaca. Every real existence reproduces the Odyssey. The path [is] toward Ithaca, toward the centre. . . . But to realize this the exile must be capable of penetrating the hidden meaning of his wanderings, and of understanding them as a long series of initiation trials (willed by the gods) and as so many obstacles on the path which brings him back to the hearth (toward the centre). That means: seeing signs, hidden meaning, symbols, in the suffering, the depressions, the dry periods in everyday life.[8] (Parentheses in original)
>
> —Mircea Eliade

8. Mircea Eliade, *Images and Symbols*, p.19.

PART II:

The Labyrinth: A Journey into the Feminine

CHAPTER FOUR: The Labyrinth Journey
CHAPTER FIVE: Reflections on the Feminine

Author at Chartres.

4

THE LABYRINTH
JOURNEY

No one need deny the danger of the descent but it can be risked. No one need risk it, but it is certain that someone will. And let those who go down the sunset way do so with open eyes, for it is a sacrifice which daunts even the Gods.[1]

—C.G. Jung

In our lifetimes, we undergo multiple journeys in and out of the center. Some are gentle, some inspiring, some chosen, some imposed, some dramatic, some challenging, some horribly painful and terrifying, some all of the above and more. The journey this book will focus on is "all of the above and more." It is the journey not much talked about and indeed often discouraged, the journey to connect with what has been in the dark. Darkness can harbor either what has been too painful to acknowledge, or hidden treasure being kept safe from forces that could destroy it. A journey into the dark can entail facing our own destructive (both to self

1. C. G. Jung, *Collected Works 5*, par. 553.

and other) capabilities—rage, hatred, jealousy, and judgment—as well as acknowledging and dealing with others' conscious or unconscious destructive feelings and acts toward us. Equally important, it can connect us with our repressed talents, with our latent creativity, and the open, loving hearts that are our birthright. The more we work with our inner demons, the more we open ourselves to the larger story of who we really are and what we can become. When such a journey is undertaken, it embraces the physical, psychological, archetypal, and spiritual dimensions of our being.

For women, the journey is even more complex. For thousands of years women have been told that living from their Feminine selves was wrong and evil. To dare to experience life from those places was tantamount to having oneself committed as insane. This happened for an uncountable number of women. Depression was a common diagnosis. Why wouldn't women be depressed when the essence of who we were was seen as unacceptable, and the opportunity to greet life from a passionate and embodied stance was taken away at every turn. It was not so long ago that women were hospitalized or confined to prolonged bed rest to not overstress our sensitive nervous systems. Patriarchal culture was so threatened and terrified by Feminine energy that it did everything in its power to control it, and the women who lived within it.

The threat included women controlling other women—mothers controlling their daughters, sisters controlling each other. The terror of these "dark realms" was so overpowering and ingrained that any sign of such a life force showing through was met with a negative response from mothers. The basis for the response was twofold. First there was the desire to protect a daughter from society's wrath, but also allowing the daughter to live on unchecked would confront the mother with the pain of her own unlived life. Women learned systems of survival and passed the knowledge down through generation after generation. Women learned to wield power, often connected to sexuality, in subtle and manipulative ways, while at the same time giving the appearance of having no power at all.

The Pattern Keeper

If my mother hadn't hated her own body
she would have shown mine compassion
instead of anger

If my mother hadn't hated her own body
she might have held mine close
and pointed out the stars

She might have told me stories about
when she was green as juice in the veins of
young trees, or sung to me

Instead of singing to the floor, on her hands
and knees, going down into a
place that was too deep
for me to reach[2]

—*Dianne Joyce*

We are fortunate that over the last century much of this has
changed, at least in our western culture. Women are beginning to
take their place in the world and find their true voices. In the beginning women tried to be like men and wield power in the same
way. Recently more women are exploring dimensions of the true
Feminine and there is a profound longing to know ourselves in a
different way and to live a more integral life. The labyrinth journey for women involves healing not only our personal wounds but
also the wounded Feminine in all her dimensions.

The Feminine has to do with relationships, whether to the inner
self, to others, or to the Self (Soul and Spirit). If we are disconnected from ourselves, we live a life bereft of authentic juiciness.
If we experience disjointed and painful relationships, our suffering
can be intense. Perhaps the most distressing level of disconnection
is to feel a severance from Spirit and the dimensions beyond.

This chapter will explore the parameters of the journey. Two

2. *Windsor Review* (University of Windsor) Vol. 33, No. 2 (2000), p. 92.

words have commonly been used to describe it. The first word is *descent* and the second is *regression*. Descent is generally the term used when speaking of the mythic archetypal level; that is, descent to the cave of the Great Goddess, or descent to the underworld or the belly of the whale. Regression has more psychological connotations and describes the process of going back to earlier states of development where we have gotten wounded or stuck.

The two processes are not mutually exclusive, and because they are intertwined true transformation and healing can occur. If we are reductive and deal with just the psychological level, we get stuck in a very small story, albeit a painful and gripping one. If we focus only on the archetypal dimension we run the risk of avoiding the healing inherent in facing personal wounding. By combining the mythic and archetypal levels of the descent with the particulars of our personal human history, we move beyond our little stories and constellate healing on many more levels.

The events that can precipitate such a journey are present in every life. Sometimes we are catapulted into it by trauma suffered in the outside world. Sometimes there is a long-standing, ever-present pain we seem unable to escape. We may know the pain in bodily symptoms, disturbing dreams, emotions of emptiness, lifelessness, or inability to create, move forward, have intimate relationships, or ever be satisfied. We may seem haunted by something we can't quite name, describe, or really even know.

At this point we have a choice, although I know it is not as simplistic as the following words might indicate. We can embark on a healing journey or we can direct our energy into diversions and addictions. Often we begin with the latter until we find it gets us nowhere. Taking the healing journey involves working on ourselves physically, emotionally, and spiritually. It is the most painful, joyous, and intriguing challenge life has to offer and takes great courage. All aspects of this journey can be a time of intense creative output, recording dreams, writing in journals, composing poetry and stories, painting images, sculpting inner figures, or dancing out feelings.

Once we embark, a personal mystery drama unfolds and we discover our inner cast of characters and their ongoing roles in our lives. This journey takes great courage, and in the midst of it we can question if we will survive the process. Painful healing on a personal and psychological level is accompanied by an opening to the spiritual and archetypal dimension. The ongoing dance between personal and spiritual leads to opening of the heart and deep empathy for the vagaries of the human condition. We begin to live our lives from a place of compassion rather than fear. We move from a place of inner power rather than being driven by a craving for power over others.

Descent: The Mythic Archetypal Level

Myths are archetypal stories about gods and goddesses—supernatural beings who open us to patterns of human development and connect us with ancient cultures. These stories are always larger than life, that is, mythic, and full of adventure and fantasy. Many were recorded in the form of epic poems that are still read today. Fairy tales, believed to be even older than myths, are about ordinary human beings, kings and queens, and have been passed down to us by word of mouth. In the last several centuries they have been committed to paper. Cross-cultural studies have shown similar themes appearing all over the planet.

Often an initiation process is described. Our forebears underwent initiation rites as a part of their maturation process—for puberty, incorporation into secret societies, marriage, and especially rites to connect with the source of Spirit and the mysteries of life and death. These rites involved a personal descent to and return from the underworld, in order to gain healing wisdom that the initiate could then share in the upper world. Although this journey used to be reserved for the traditional shaman or medicine man or woman, many modern people are finding themselves either willingly or unwillingly undergoing wisdom initiation. It speaks of the spiritual readiness of so many of us to bring deep healing energy to our communities, our planet, and ourselves.

If we use the labyrinth as a model, the initiation process generally involves a descent to the underworld (in to the center), time spent in the underworld where death and rebirth happen (the center itself), and then a return to the upper world (away from the center).

A well-known story line for this epic is the Hero's journey. The late Joseph Campbell delineated stages of the Hero's journey as follows. First, there is the call, which when responded to leads to meeting the guardians at the threshold. Our readiness is confirmed once we are allowed to cross over and encounter both tests and allies. The center is where the Hero meets and slays the "monster." (The monster can be seen as something outside of us that exudes danger, evokes terror, and must be eliminated at all costs, but is in fact a projection of something from deep within.) Once this happens, the Hero wins the "boon" and makes his way back to the upper world with a treasure.

The Hero's story is in our bones. We have absorbed it with our mother's milk. You must be strong and slay the monster before it slays you. That is the only way to ultimate freedom. Even as a young girl I remember identifying with that story from all the books and movies I devoured. It didn't matter to me that the hero was a man. I was going to be a hero too and conquer evil. Sometimes it is important to be heroic and stand up to evil. The difficulty with this story, which we shall see clearly in the myth of Theseus (Chapter 6) and Inanna (Chapter 8), is that nothing is learned from the monster who has been killed, except we know for a moment in time that we were stronger than it was. How much of that drama is being enacted in our world situation today?

The transformation begins when we acknowledge that the monster is actually a part of us. What becomes exceedingly important on a deeper stage of the journey is daring to be in the presence of this monster. The journey to the center of the labyrinth, the monster's abode, is often a path on which to build strength and courage in order to face the monster and survive. Timing is everything. If we push too hard, walls of defense become thicker and stronger. If we allow the journey to progress at its own pace, safety, trust, and strength are built, and the story can unfold.

Once we accept the fact that this monster is a part of ourselves, we need to cultivate an attitude of curiosity toward it. Who is it?

What is it? How did it come into being? What does it need from me? What do I need from it? Is it a part of me that I need to let go of? Is it a part that needs to be integrated? We are often shocked to discover how much pain this part might be in, how much rage it might hold, and how it has wreaked havoc in our lives because we have not paid attention to it.

The Hero's way is *one* way but not the *only* way. It is a way to reconnect with a certain level of our strength and power *over* others, which is sometimes very necessary, but not with the depth of power that comes from knowing who we really are. Although many stages of the journey are similar, there is a difference when we follow the Feminine way. Myths from this perspective involve profound suffering and often a lot of waiting. When the suffering of the Feminine is known and acknowledged, release from suffering is possible. With the release comes an inner strength and power and an opening of the heart that cannot be taken away.

Regression: The Psychological Level

Most of us carry a wounded child around inside. Like all children, this child wants our attention. When we don't pay her enough attention, she makes sure we know she is there, only we don't often realize that she is the one speaking. She has a story to tell and wants us to hear it. The story can be full of pain and hurt, but it can also express an urge to play and have fun.

When we don't pay attention to her, the wounded inner child tries to get her needs met through others. For example, when we fall in love or get into a relationship, each person brings at least two others to the table, an adult self and a child self. This is where the confusion begins. The inner child naturally opens her heart totally to the other, hoping that this time her needs will be met. If the relationship ends, she feels devastated, betrayed, and abandoned. The depth of the wounding is much more profound than what might occur between two adults. When we feel so terribly distraught, it is a message from our child saying, "Something is very wrong. I need you to listen to me. I need you to know how much I have been hurt so that you as the adult can hold me, protect me, know my vulnerabilities, and not let me get hurt again." When we begin to differentiate our adult self from our child self, we are well on our way to healing.

Where does the wounding of the child start? It can begin as early as *in utero* or in infancy. As infants we need someone else, most often mother, to mediate both between us and the outside world and our inner world of chaos. Mother holds the connection to something larger, which Jung called the Self (with a capital *S*). The Self is the "God essence" or spiritual center within a person. If a mother is connected to her own Self, she can hold the child in a space of love and safety. From a deeply-rooted center like a tree we can withstand much in our outer life. Because the wounded Feminine is passed down through the generations, it is often the case that women are not connected and can live in a chaotic world with no grounding. This gets communicated to the infant.

What happens next is part of the mystery and depends to a large degree on some of these additional factors. What is the genetic or soul structure of the infant? How will that help it to navigate a world that appears threatening and dangerous? Who else has the infant been exposed to? What other things happen as the infant develops and grows? What kinds of trauma has it had to survive—physical, psychological, or spiritual?

W. D.Winnicott, a British psychoanalyst, has coined three terms: unbearable anxiety, the good enough mother, and the true self/false self. These concepts are invaluable in our understanding of the power of regression and why it feels like such a dangerous place. He talks about "unbearable anxiety," that is, anxiety that is not bearable. If we cannot bear it what do we do? We try to do anything and everything to avoid it. If we go near this unbearable anxiety we feel it could kill us or drive us mad.

For a child these fears are true, for an adult they don't have to be. Unbearable anxiety is most often the state of an infant before language has developed and before she has the capacity to process what is happening to her. Most of you have seen infants cry hysterically and inconsolably. It is a heart-wrenching sight. When this level of crying happens repeatedly, over extended periods of time with no adult mediation, the child can be traumatized. This level of trauma gets registered in the nervous system on a basic and primitive level. We have no cognitive memories of these events but our bodies do. The same can be true of children who have suffered physical, emotional, and sexual abuse. Their bodies carry the stories and hold the terror. As we grow and mature, these stories continue to live inside of us. Events can trigger these moments of unbearable anxiety from childhood but we don't realize where the anxiety has come from. We forget that as adults we no longer need to feel terrorized. We are overwhelmed in the present moment and don't know why. Regression in a therapeutic context helps reconnect with the source of the original trauma and begin the healing process.

Winnicott also speaks of the "good enough mother." She is able to meet her baby's needs enough of the time so that the infant feels safe and contained. This is so important. If we do not have a sense that the world is potentially a safe place, we become permeated with fear. It becomes lodged in our bodies with a potential to endanger our health as we mature. It also precipitates behavior based on the premise that there is never enough, and we must grab power and look after ourselves with little regard for the consequences of our actions. This is especially strong when we feel threatened. If we feel betrayed by our personal mother, chances are we will either cling to Spirit in some form but not be grounded, or we will find it difficult to trust. Energy that could otherwise be put toward living a creative life becomes devoted to ensuring our basic survival.

As the infant gets older, it goes through a phase of feeling like it is the center of the universe and everything that happens does so because of it. If he or she continues to feel neglected and unloved the thoughts are: There is something wrong with me. I must be unlovable. I must be bad. Maybe I am so bad I can hurt other people. Maybe I am so bad, evil, dirty, ugly, or stupid, that no one will ever want to have anything to do with me again. Maybe I should never let myself get too close to someone because then they will find out that deep down inside I am really a terrible person. Maybe I should never get close, because if I am so bad I could hurt them.

These are the stories that come out when we begin the journey to our wounded places, and these are the parts that need to be healed. These ideas become detached from reality and that is precisely why they hold so much power over us. By moving through these layers of self-doubt and understanding their origins, we can connect with the true self who lives underneath. We need to learn how and why we have adopted these ideas about ourselves and that they do not indicate our true nature. We need to embrace a new view of the reality of who we are.

What do I mean by "true self"? This is where Winnicott's third term comes in. He talks about the true self and the false self. When our true self has been threatened, we develop a false self to show the world, which we hope will protect our true self from any further harm. We live inside another skin (the prince inside the frog, or the beautiful princess inside the ugly old hag) seemingly "bewitched" or under a spell. We will stay bewitched and in that false skin until we are "kissed" and loved for who we truly are.

One way we can protect ourselves is by splitting, or separating ourselves from our feelings. Living from a false self is a form of splitting, where we show a part of ourselves to the world but hold back what is more sacred and precious. This can lead to a sense of feeling unreal. We can also split horizontally, by moving up into our heads and cutting ourselves off from any feeling in our bodies. The third split is a side-to-side split, where we exhibit two very distinct ways of being in the world that may conflict with each other. We may have one personality that is shy and introverted, and another that is outgoing and extroverted and have difficulty reconciling the two.

Another way we protect ourselves is to dissociate. I was watching the movie *Annie Hall* one night and there was a perfect example. Annie Hall and the Woody Allen character are making love. Normally, she has to smoke a joint in order to relax, but this time he convinces her not to. As soon as he touches her, she leaves her body. There she is sitting on a chair observing herself, and at the same time she is in bed with him. He says to her, "I don't feel you are here." So true. When the addiction that normally helped her to deal with anxiety wasn't used, she figuratively left. This is another common form of self-protection. We "leave" our bodies because it is too painful to stay in them. Thus we live our lives as observers rather than participants.

Part of our journey to the center of the labyrinth can involve going back to places of unbearable anxiety. The labyrinth, as a model of the therapeutic regression process, teaches us a lot about doing this with great care and awareness. We must slowly build a sense of trust, not only in our ability to survive such a descent but also in the capacity of the one accompanying us to go there with us. Hopefully it is someone who can hold both the personal and archetypal realities.

With the personal and archetypal perspectives in mind, let's look at how this journey might be played out with the labyrinth model. We begin with the call, then make the journey in, spend time in the center, and end with the trip of return.

The Call, Allies and Guardians at the Threshold

There are two ways of entering the underworld. We either make a conscious choice to respond to the call like Inanna and Theseus, or we can be "raped" into the underworld the way Persephone was. (Part III will discuss these myths in depth.) Most of us experience both the chosen and unchosen descent in our lifetimes.

The call often begins very softly. Many of us try to ignore it until we have no choice but to listen. It can be an irritating, nagging feeling that says what we have is not enough. It can be a feeling of dissatisfaction, an inner realization that there is something we need to do but don't know quite what. It can be a remembering of some childhood purpose or mission. Synchronistic events in life can signal such a call. The call comes from Soul, urging us on in our personal process of individuation. It can be a call to deepen into Spirit, rediscover and embody repressed talents, heal wounded parts of ourselves, and be of service.

We ignore the call at our peril. I have heard many stories of people who have heard the call to change their lives, but for a variety of reasons chose not to pay attention. We may begin by ignoring an inner knowing that we are being called to do something or learn something. If we persist in not paying attention, what can follow are warnings—an illness, an unconscious error, a near accident. If we continue to ignore these signs the ante can be upped and we can be faced with more life-threatening circumstances. Something is trying to get our attention and we are not listening. When we are not paying attention nightmares can point to what our unconscious might have been gently trying to communicate.

If we answer the call and cross the threshold, there is no turning back. On a train journey in New Zealand I met a man who told me an incredible story. Like a good mystery the story unfolded bit by bit, over the eight hours we spent together. He had been part of a religious order in his youth and had left, pursued a career, gotten married, and fathered a son. At some point, his sexual orientation became clear to him and he left the marriage, the son, and his wife. Still not feeling right with the world, he began to take spiritual direction and felt the call to rejoin his old religious order. With the encouragement of his spiritual director, he reapplied. There were very rigorous criteria involved in the reentry process. He had to dispose of his worldly goods and make some very painful and irrevocable changes in his personal and family relationships. He was certain he was hearing God's call and threw himself into the process wholeheartedly. You can guess what happened. The guardians at this particular threshold, the religious order's selection committee, refused to admit him. The shock was immense. He was taking this train journey in an attempt to come to terms with what had happened. His most pressing question was how he could have misunderstood his call.

Had he really misunderstood or had the process unfolded exactly as it should? The committee's refusal became a test that threw him into an even deeper experience of himself in relation to the sacred, one he would not have had otherwise. We never know at what stage of the journey profound lessons will come. Being refused passage across a threshold in our lives feels devastating in the moment. Often with hindsight, we can see that the refusal may have changed our direction in a way that was much more in line with what we really were meant to be doing.

I have found in my own life that once I have crossed the threshold and am truly on the path, allies abound. People will come into my life for a short time or a long time, but with significant impact. They might introduce me to another person, a book, an event, or support me through a difficult transition. Once the same spiritual teacher was brought to my attention by three different people within weeks of each other. I listened.

Allies also come from within. When we begin to listen to ourselves and trust our own intuition and feelings—that still small voice within—we can become our own most profound and important ally.

What happens when we are plummeted into the underworld against our will and seemingly random events shatter the veil of illusion we live under? When I was fifteen, my grandfather died suddenly of a stroke. When I was eighteen, an automobile accident killed three young men from my community. Death was staring me in the eye and I could not look away. The ground disappeared from beneath my feet and I tumbled into a dark, uncompromising pit. For months I could not get my bearings. How could someone be here one day and gone the next? I felt like I was drowning in the existential mysteries of human life and there were no satisfactory answers.

Every day we hear stories in the news of such events: a woman walking her dog is killed by a drunk driver, a scaffolding breaks and falls on a pedestrian walking underneath, young people are at a party and one gets beaten and dies. On a human level it is impossible to comprehend. We need to take the time to mourn our losses, rage at the inequity, and sink into our personal spiritual crisis. The energy of the dark strikes again, leaving us unbalanced and unhooked.

Sometimes the plummeting is not so random. We can be faced with a life-threatening illness either in ourselves or a loved one. We can suffer abandonment either from the breakup of relationships or death. We can be fired from a job. We can lose all our possessions in a fire. We can be assaulted, raped, or robbed. Each of these events serves as a catalyst, plunging us into the underworld, often into the Dark Night of the Soul as described by

St. John of the Cross; that is, complete loss of spiritual connection and a sense of abandonment by God.

The Journey In

If we are not dropped into the underworld, we can undergo the slow journey down that is symbolized by the labyrinth. This does not mean the journey is now a smooth one. We are still being prepared. We still follow the forward and backward movement of the labyrinth and move between the quadrants. In a sense, we are being strengthened at the same time that we are being stripped. Our defenses are broken down, our images of ourselves shattered, our place on the earth questioned.

The rhythm of the journey might look like this. We feel badly. We allow ourselves to experience pain. An insight comes and we have a small breakthrough. We feel better. We move forward until the next event sends us backward again. In essence, the disturbances of our daily lives serve this purpose. They keep us on the edge and always moving. At some point, when we are strong enough, we might be grabbed by a depression we cannot seem to shake. This is the call to stay put, to look inward, to be present in the dark. We awaken to our inner anguish and to the depth of sorrow in the world. Our suffering opens our minds, strips us of our usual *modus operandi*, and awakens us to the most profound of human journeys. This is where we move from being victims of our fate to being pilgrims on a path. The myth of Inanna (Chapter 9) gives us a wonderful model for this part of the journey.

The Center

At first we have to stay with our suffering without hope of change. We do not know it, but endurance itself provides us with the weight to bear the next steps.[3]

3. John Tarrant, *The Light Inside the Dark*, p. 40.

The center is not the goal but a way station along the path. When our descent into the dark feels like more than we can bear, we tend to forget this. We drop into an abyss and darkness is all the eye can see. It is the place of no hope and no light. Being there is excruciating, and at the same time it is the place of no pain. We can feel like a dormant pruned tree going into winter, not knowing if we will survive to grow leaves again in the spring. The eyes through which we see the world brim over with sorrow and a sense of desolation. We are in the void . . . waiting.

Here we encounter ourselves without sham and meet ourselves coming back to ourselves. As filtered light penetrates the shadows, that which has lain dormant for eons becomes known and we sit in its presence. We take a broom to the hidden corners, investigating what has been concealed in the dust.

From an archetypal perspective, we know this is where we meet the Dark Goddess and her realm. We meet her in her love and compassion but also in her ruthlessness. Her compassion is fierce and we are there to learn from her. The Goddess of Life and Death brooks no dissent. Her realm is one of absolutes. We know her mythologically through the goddesses Inanna, Kali, and Durga, through the witches Baba Yaga and the Hag (See Chapter 6). She is Le-Hev-Hev of the Malekula, who demanded that each soul draw the labyrinth pattern correctly or they would not enter her Queendom.

We can not travel to the dark realm unless we also know we are held in the embrace of a compassionate energy, and know ourselves as the adults we truly are. Only then can we safely re-experience the unbearable anxiety of our wounded inner child. As children we may have known that light of Spirit, and were often told by adults around us not to be silly, so we closed that part of ourselves down. We need to bear witness to the stories long kept hidden and give space for the emotional purging that can accompany them.

We cannot fight our way out as the hero does. The more one fights, the further away what one is fighting for seems to get. We need to swim in the ocean of our beingness, divesting ourselves of what is no longer helpful while awaiting the moment when we are ready to emerge born anew.

Danger is also in this central place, for it is where madness can lie. Mad "pockets" in sane people can be related to states of unbearable anxiety and unacknowledged trauma of the infant. Splitting and dissociation are ways we have developed to protect ourselves. When stripped of those defenses in the center, we are open to our madness. This is why we need to take great care and follow the parameters of the journey carefully. This will be explored in more depth in the myth of Inanna (Chapter 8).

A colleague shared with me an incident from a particularly painful and frightening time. He had fluctuated between mania and depression, and knew he was close to going "over the edge," as he put it. Then he had a vision. He saw in front of him a door, and behind the door was the most wonderful, beckoning light. He was drawn toward it when, to his amazement, he "knew" that if he went through that door he would never come back. This message seemed to have been written across the front of the door, warning him. He took the warning very seriously, sought help for his difficulties, and probably saved his own life.

The following poem gives a sense of the madness we might meet, as we symbolically enter the center of the labyrinth.

Shattered

Shattered
She flails about
A madwoman in a room of precious things.
Unjointed
Her limbs fly wild
And nothing is safe.

Hurling words like chaff
Against the walls
Already pitted and scarred,
She crashes
Into fairy tale mirrors and the fragile glass
Of dreams,
Her feet bleeding on the carpet
Of her own illusions.

The knob is gone from the door.
No where to turn
But round and round
And round
She spins inward
A madwoman
Journeying
Home.[4]

—*Jayelle Lindsay*

Leaving the Center

There is a remarkable passage in the novel *Alice's Masque* by
Lindsay Clarke that gives us a sense of the depth of the center
and the perturbations we feel when it is time to leave. It is the
labyrinth journey on returning to the outside with all its twists
and turns. The story is about the descent of a man to the realm
of the Hag—a representative of the primal Feminine—to
learn what the Feminine is. It describes beautifully and evoca-
tively the beginning of the slow journey out of a place of total
vulnerability.

> Another way stands open. Its tall stair winds ahead of him, and
> the effort of the climb will take him up and out. That way he
> can pass back through the veil of matter. He can pick up the
> human task again. He can resume the dance . . .
>
> He takes the first steps upwards. Imagination gathers speed,
> accelerating back through all the kingdoms of the beasts and he
> remembers himself capable of more than howls. Hoarsely the
> breath in his throat takes the shape of words. As he climbs, he
> staggers back into the limitless possibilities of language, as-
> tounded and delighted by the trickery of names, those loops of
> light that ring and dazzle towards him. He wonders at their
> countless spells to conjure, shrivel, bless, at their capacity for
> making play, at all the tongue's infatuating weaponry.

4. Jayelle Lindsay, *Tangible Evidence*, p. 49.

We see here the struggle to integrate and reclaim the human self, but in a new way. As he spirals upward through the layers of collective and personal history, he begins to see the world through new eyes. That which previously terrified him now delights and gives strength.

> Soon there comes a time of images within images, for he is in touch with a prolific and far-ranging intelligence which contemplates other pictures, other scenes, even as it follows his progress up the winding stair. At each complete turn of the spiral it finds no difficulty in conceiving how his existence has been wound on a generation, from the earliest, most primitive of men, through long millennia, until he is in the time and experience of a maze-dancing people far removed from what had recently been his own monolithic mode of consciousness. He is astonished how spacious their world, how widely its bounds of meaning reach to embrace the planets and the stars. And still the stairs twist upwards drawing him on through the pattern of his ancestry till he is in his great-grandfather's time, then his grandfather's, and his father's—where he approaches the passionate moment when his present life will be conceived.
>
> At that point he reaches the last skin of rock that stands between this inner and outer world. The sounds around him merge into the clamour of the waterfall. He sees that he has arrived at a place inside the wall of rock that forms fall's wild cell. He smiles with recognition, remembering how—not long ago, and from the other side—that very place had filled his mind with dread. Now he can delight in its no longer alien intelligence. He draws strength from it.[5]

The Way Out

Once we have spent our time in the center, letting light into the dark places, knowing the dark places, and finally transforming the dark places, it is time to move back into the world. Often we have

5. Lindsay Clarke, *Alice's Masque*, pp. 214–216.

to wait until we have regrown our skin, so well described in the previous passage. In the center we have been open and vulnerable. How can we emerge, still be open to ourselves, but also protect ourselves in a world that moves quickly and does not recognize vulnerability? The journey out follows the same path as the journey in for this reason. It gives us the time we need to build our strength and integrate what has been learned.

Using the labyrinth as a model, it becomes very clear that the journey out will not be straightforward. It is hard work with times of progression and regression as we struggle to integrate the new with the old and to truly heal. It sometimes takes years for certain fears to gradually dissipate and the new "knowing" ourselves to become integrated in such a way that it becomes the norm. One day, we suddenly realize that we are no longer afraid.

A recent example came from a client who has struggled for years with a terror of speaking out in groups. She would only risk it when the energy was so strong inside of her that she felt she had no choice. After she spoke, she would fall into a pit of self recrimination and despair. How could she have betrayed herself by risking so much? On a deeper level, she felt she would be annihilated for showing her true self. In our work together, she followed the tortuous path down to reveal a history of severe emotional abuse and a true self hidden safely in its cave. Her healing process was complex, profound, and lengthy. Being a student, her fears of speaking were constantly being challenged, but she was slowly gaining confidence. One day she came into a session beaming. She had found herself speaking out in a group and only afterward did she realize it had just come naturally. There was no angst before or after. She was thrilled and so was I. In terms of that particular complex, something had been healed. The labyrinthe journey had been worth it.

We become conscious that our inner child is triggered when we find ourselves reacting in ways inappropriate to the reality of the present moment. Some indicators can be the intensity or duration of our feelings. We often get a sense that our grief or rage is disproportionate to the situation we are facing, or that the feelings are lasting too long. Clients will come back to me and say, "I thought of you when a setback happened and when I asked myself the question, 'How old do you feel now?' I realized I was 5, or 2, or even an infant, and was able to put things into a different perspective." The client was able, in the moment, to recognize the presence of her wounded child and to hold it lovingly. Once this begins to happen we are on the road to breaking the spell of the complex and integrating the healing we have experienced in the center of the labyrinth.

How much of our lives have been lived under these spells of the past? As they are burned away, a new consciousness takes over. The journey down and the time in the center awakens us to our underlying misperceptions and woundings that have haunted us. We need to stay connected to what we have learned in life. The simplest and most profound way to do that is to remember to breathe. When we get caught in our complexes we stop breathing, and in so doing we retraumatize ourselves and continue to be the victim. When we breathe, we remember our connection to the larger story—who we really are, how old we are, how much we know. When we breathe, we can differentiate between present-day reality for our adult selves and the no-longer-relevant reality of the wounded child in the present circumstances.

We have heard the child's story. We know her wounds and her terrors. It is now up to us to protect her, for ultimately we are the one she must rely on. In the beginning others teach us how to protect ourselves and we are grateful for their help, but they cannot be there all the time. Others are also human with their own inner child issues and sometimes their priorities take over. In the adult world that is right. Our inner child must become our priority. We must learn how to listen to her and to be able to differentiate between when things are too much for her and when she needs to be pushed a little. We need to ascertain when we are strong enough to face situations that were previously terrifying. We need to learn to make a distinction between situations of actual danger and when we have fallen under the old spell.

As I was writing this chapter, I came across Don Miguel Ruiz's *The Four Agreements*, in which the author delineates four agreements we must make in order to live a life unbounded and free.

We must undertake this work as we emerge from the center of the labyrinth and begin the process of integrating our healed selves into the outer world. What he says comes from the ancient Toltec wisdom and echoes the ancient wisdom of many traditions. The four agreements are: 1. Be impeccable with your word. 2. Never take anything personally. 3. Don't make assumptions 4. Always do your best.[6]

His first agreement is to *be impeccable with your word*. This is simple and at the same time complex. When we gossip and speak negatively about others, we are reinforcing the poisoned belief system that there is something wrong with us and with them. If we think negatively about others, without a doubt we think negatively about ourselves. Watch yourself. See how often you want to share a perception of another that is not complimentary or puts him or her down. Become aware of what a struggle it is to let go of that urge. It really is a struggle. We rationalize with all kinds of statements, such as: I am just trying to understand them better, or explore my feelings, or get some feedback (all of which might be true to some extent). But what about our responsibility for contributing to the negative energy surrounding another person just by putting those words out? We need to always bring it back to us, not in a sense of blame but in a sense of compassion.

Ruiz's second agreement is *never take anything personally*. For most of us this is a real challenge. When our wounded child gets triggered, we take everything personally. We are sure that the world is giving us confirmation that we are indeed bad, evil, ugly, or dangerous, and this throws us back into the pit of living hell from which we have been struggling so hard to escape. Having spent time in the center, in the presence of these dark aspects, we have come to know them and can now put them in a different context. We see how they originated, how we identified with them and used them. We see their truth. We see they no longer serve us.

We also become aware of how others are operating from their inner wounded children. The wounding things they do to us may

6. Don Miguel Ruiz, *The Four Agreements*.

have more to do with themselves and their misperceptions of the situation than with us. We begin to be able to separate ourselves from the intensity of the emotion and view the situation from a more objective stance.

I had a seminal experience of this several years ago. I had gotten into an altercation with some women with whom I had been organizing an event. As the date of the event approached, our disagreement intensified. At the eleventh hour, they very responsibly completed their commitment to the process, then announced they would not attend the event. I was devastated. At first, I was angry with them. Then, I was very angry with myself and felt guilty for my part in the drama. Unable to sleep that night, I stayed with the feelings and began peeling back the layers. As I shed each set of false assumptions both about them and myself, I was able to go beyond my vindictiveness and recrimination until I reached a place of stillness. In that space, my heart opened and I realized how much I loved those women and how shattered I was that we were no longer able to communicate. I had arrived at the essence, and although painful, it was a resting place.

The above example is also addressed by Don Miguel Ruiz's third agreement, *don't make assumptions*. We walk around feeling there is only one way to see the world, *our way*. As a result, we project our personal interpretation of events onto others and assume our truth is also their truth.

I have another story. Before giving my first lecture for the Jung Society in Toronto, I lived in a state of terror. I didn't quite understand where it was coming from, but it was so incapacitating I was having difficulty finishing the writing. One day, I was speaking with Marion Woodman on the phone, and in her inimitable, direct manner she said to me, "Well, Sylvia, you can choose to project your negative mother on to the audience or not!" That woke me up. I had unconsciously assumed that everyone in the audience would be holding the same negative mother energy I held inside, and would only see everything I did wrong. I was not aware I was holding that assumption, and letting it go allowed me to approach the lecture with a great deal more equanimity. It went well.

Ruiz's final agreement is *always do your best*. Doing our best means staying connected to the depth of who we are. It means using our consciousness to work through situations and finally come to the resting place in our integrity and our open hearts.

This is the challenge of our times. How do we stay present and hold the opposites of rage and love, sorrow and joy, and stay connected to our spiritual and human center? How can we each be a beacon in the world that shines with the light of compassion and at the same time takes action to right inequities? As human beings we are being called upon to stretch in ways that confront our core views of the world and ourselves. The more conscious we become, the more courage we will have. The more we meet each other with eyes wide open, the more we begin to change.

Canadian poet Dianne Joyce speaks of this necessary journey for healing by going into the hidden and wounded in ourselves.

What Is Hidden in Myself

Today the runes told me
my time is up, That I must now
wait, go inside, look for the thing
hidden: what I've been reluctant
to admit to the clear light of day.

This is the time of initiation
And darkness.

I imagine myself near a stone altar
in another country, wearing white.
Imagine that I must pay
for some wrong suffered—
it is the way of things:

A test from the goddess, a walk through
the labyrinth. Only then will I be ready
for my journey.[7]

---

7. Unpublished poem.

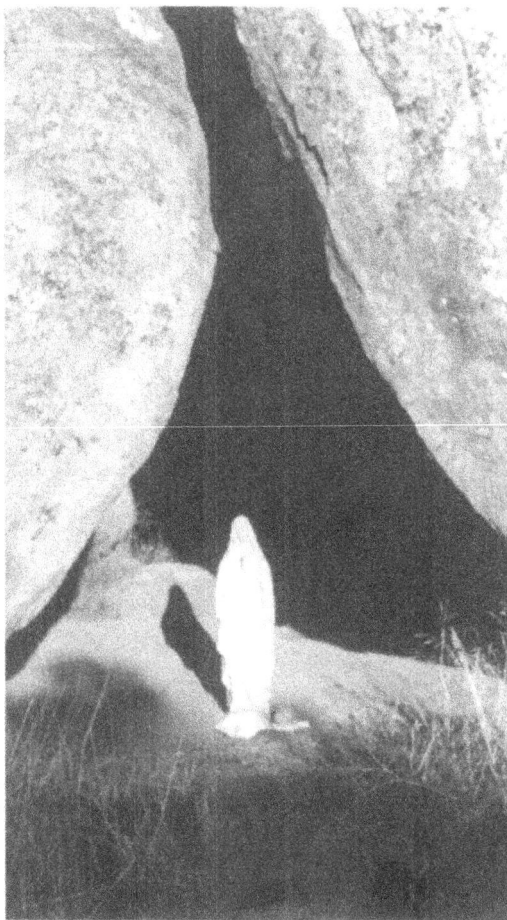

Statue in the rocks, Southern California.

5

REFLECTIONS
ON THE FEMININE

*It took me an awfully long time to honour the animal in me,
to see that my most vital part could be messy, and violent
and full of fury. That it had a perfect right to those feelings,
and needed to shriek and rampage far more than I'd ever
dared to let it do.*

And what happened when you did? (asks another character)

*Trouble, of course. But I was already in trouble anyway. I
just didn't know how to make it work for me.*[1]

— Lindsay Clarke, *Alice's Masque*

The labyrinth journey is the journey of the Feminine. What does
that really mean? What is the Feminine? What are the images of
the Feminine that are seizing the imagination of women today? In
order to find out, I began to listen. I listened to myself, my
dreams, and what my writing revealed. I listened as the hesitant
voices of women sounded through their dreams, poetry, art,

---

1. Lindsay Clarke, *Alice's Masque*, p. 18.

music, and dance. I began to notice more books by women trying to express, define, and understand the inner images and sensations that informed their lives. I listened as these women struggled with believing in themselves enough to share their experiences with others, and I saw how tentative that was at first. I listened to the terror that often accompanied revelations of the Feminine voice, and to the courage it took for women to express themselves from those deep places within.

This chapter is an exploration of the Feminine interspersed with dreams and poetry. It will look at both light and dark aspects of the Feminine. In exploring the dark, we will differentiate between what is unknown and waiting to be brought to consciousness, from that which wants to destroy life and can consume us with negativity. We will examine the Feminine in her primordial, archetypal, divine, and human aspects, remembering that we meet and know this energy when we walk the labyrinth.

The Primordial Feminine

While training in Zurich I read *The Symbolic Quest* by Edward Whitmont and was stunned by the quote below. It spoke about aspects of what I had learned in my river experience, and the mystery of the Feminine I had intuited. It also speaks to my sense of being connected with an ancient Primordial Feminine presence from the caves of the Great Goddess while walking the labyrinth. The quote is by Linda Fierz David, an analyst who worked with Jung. She describes a Yin energy that endlessly conceives, births volcanically, and at the same time is in a state of inertia. The energy is nonhuman and nonspiritual, yet paradoxically has profound wisdom. She imagines the dark Feminine as a force struggling to make itself known to those who are prepared to listen. This quote is dense, speaks of forces many of us may not have experienced, and may need to be read several times. She starts as follows:

> As always when one interprets, one tends easily to idealize and, in this instance, to visualize *Yin the Receptive* as something akin

to loving motherliness. We start with the mother image in order to actualize the Feminine principle, but this is just what we must not do because the Feminine is the opposite of the Spiritual and the ideal. *Yin* is the mother-womb of the Soul, conceiving and giving birth. Whatsoever falls therein is borne, ripens and is ejected, regardless. It is the ever bearing, but also the inert. In conceiving, it remains indifferent, cold, and unseeing. It stays immovably on the spot; only in giving birth does it shake and quake like the irrational volcano.

It is in one sense really quite hazardous to realize this, for though the deeply Feminine is the center from which all psychic life pours forth, just because of its vast inertia it is inimically opposed to all action, all consciousness and development. Just as outer nature, without man's intervention, ceaselessly creates and destroys in unconcerned and senseless continuation, allowing fruits to ripen and decay and animals to live and die, so the Feminine without the active intervention of the conscious mind proceeds on an undisciplined and ever life-productive way. [2]

Fierz David begins by disabusing us of any sentimentality regarding the Feminine. If we conceptualize it as a *primordial* energy, this is helpful. It is a force concerned with the continuation of life including giving birth, ripening, decay and death. The Feminine is nature without human intervention as it grows wild by following its own rhythm. It is like a rampaging forest fire whose heat releases new growth. When women give birth they are in the throes of Her energy. In sexual passion we know this energy. When we dance ecstatically we can be filled with it. Because of its uncontrollable nature and lack of consciousness, it has been feared by both men and women. Most of us are terrified of losing control. The terror of this unknown force is at the base of the strictures of patriarchy. Some boundaries are necessary, but patriarchy is an example of the masculine gone overboard in its attempts to subdue that which it cannot command.

2. Linda Fierz David in Edward C. Whitmont, *The Symbolic Quest*, pp. 172–173.

The Feminine is not the primitive, for the primitive contains a relative amount of consciousness and development; it is rather the non-human and non-spiritual. The awesome point is that this non-Spirituality, this non-humanity, is yet a wellspring for human experience, similar to an ancient, sluggish beast which has watched man for thousands of years and now knows everything, long before it occurs. It is for us an almost insulting paradox that the non-Spiritual should be wise, but thus it is. This wisdom is not friendly to man for it never suits a particular time or person but relates solely to the stark, raw everlasting of the unconscious psychic life; and just as organic life never remains static, but goes on relentlessly—ever renewing even the organism in the single cell—so the Feminine encompasses the whole vibrant ever-new rhythm of psychic activity, the inescapable change of every hardened form. Thus it contains and destroys all in one. It is unswerving stability and terrifying breakdown. It expresses itself in the sexual demands, in the adaptability of instincts, in shattering emotions, and because of its wayward uncontrollability, in a truly devilish wisdom.[3]

What has captivated my imagination is the idea of an ancient, wise, all-knowing, earth-connected beast. I imagine it in its cave, watching and being, as we tap into its profound knowing in our own psyches and in the collective energy of the planet. It holds all paradox by containing and destroying all in one. It is nonhuman; therefore we cannot know it with our conscious minds, but only through our bodies, senses, and dreams. It is the wellspring of our authentic creativity. It appears when we play around and allow the mystery of creative inspiration to speak through us. If we let it, the beast pushes the boundaries of the old and allows the new to emerge.

In her inmost being every woman is moved by this Feminine principle of *Yin*. Aside from all she says or does, aside from her most intimate bond to people and Spiritual values, it expresses

3. Ibid.

itself in her as something strange and foreign, something "other" that unmistakably goes its own way.

Here she is pushed beyond any need of her own, or the needs of her nearest and dearest, by the compelling necessity of this rhythm. Here she does not recognize outer time and its demands but only the unmistakable signs of an inner ebb and flow. Quite unconsciously and involuntarily this deepest part of her is concerned only with the growth and maturing of life which demands its rights, must demand its rights, whether she wishes it or not.[4]

How often do women not understand their feelings and behavior? There is a sense of following a mysterious rhythm based on biology and hormones, but it is stronger, deeper, and larger than that.

This is what fundamentally makes women so mysterious to themselves as well as to others. The *Yin* in them demands the inexplicable and unknowable, pushes on to the next step in the unknown part of life, adds the yet unconscious part to the consciously known, and finds in every situation the germ of the new. It is therefore inexpressible and all words and explanations can only give an artificial and untrue picture. This great darkness pregnant with life is the reality. *To us that darkness seems suspect and morbid and we turn away from it whenever possible.* Therefore the vibrant, living darkness of *Yin* is seldom recognized in its essential meaning by modern cultured women, *in its natural expression of impulsive feelings and emotions which could contact the unknown depths of consciousness.* Or if it is perceived at all, it is quickly thrust away under the cover of convictions, opinions, concepts and rationalizations that misconstrue and twist the mystery even as it emerges into being. That which could be understood by experiencing is cut off, crippled even in embryo. Then the deep substratum of the stream of psychic life is blocked, dammed up, and it floods over in moments of unguarded unconsciousness, in overpowering

4. Ibid.

affects that disturb and twist the meaning of everything around it. Or the *Yin* inserts itself slyly in the conscious and unconscious intrigues and suspicions of women with which they unwittingly poison themselves and those around them.[5] (italics mine)

Trying to describe something while limited by words is a challenge. Fierz David is telling us we know this Feminine force when we allow it to pulse through us, and when we are inexplicably overcome with emotions so deep and powerful we are shocked because we are not used to living from that place. My experience at the river is an example of this energy speaking through me. By turning away from it, we block its expression and our connection becomes severed. It then comes out in "overpowering affects that destroy and twist meaning," intrigues and suspicions through which women "unwittingly poison themselves and those around them." We need to differentiate the energy of the dark Feminine that is distorted, negative, destructive, and "bitchy," from the energy of the Feminine grounded in primordial depths and who speaks from that place.

As I was writing this, I heard the news of a suicide bomb attack in a Jerusalem restaurant that killed at least fifteen people (including six children), and injured ninety. This kind of news, no matter who the victims are, brings out that Feminine energy in me. I want to go over there, assume my eleven-mile-high power stance, shake them all, and scream at the top of my lungs, "Stop it!" This is the Primordial Feminine speaking out for life. What would happen if women gathered together and did just that? What if from the power of our knowing we stood together and said "No more!"? This is the message I believe the Feminine is sending to us. She wants us to wake up, move out of our inertia, and act for Her. That is even more true after the events of September 11th, 2001, and our subsequent engagement in war.

5. Ibid.

The Feminine and Inertia

Putting together the idea of inertia with constant birthing was confusing to me until I had the following conversation with a client. She was speaking about her growing spiritual awareness and need to change her form of worship. For years she had been a regular church-goer but it no longer served her. In spite of that, she found it difficult to break the habit of regular attendance. I suddenly realized that here is an example of inertia. When we continue to do the same thing over and over because we don't have the energy to change, we are caught in the inertia of the Feminine. We realized together that only a conscious act in the world (Masculine energy) would be able to break through the inertia and move her into another space. The definition of *inertia* supports this view, as the property of a body that remains at rest or continues moving in a straight line unless acted upon by a directional force.

One form of inertia can keep us locked in patterns of behavior. Another form of inertia is a part of the process of connection with the dark Feminine discussed in Chapter 4. Once we descend into the dark, we may need to stay there for a period of time in the presence of the Primordial Feminine until we have learned what we need to. (See Chapter 7 on Demeter and Persephone, and Chapter 8 on Inanna.) We wait there until we know what, where, or how to act. For many of us, these states can be terrifying and very uncomfortable. However, like the seed that needs to incubate in the ground until it is the right time to sprout, so we too need to lie dormant, waiting. If the work goes deep enough, redeeming our Feminine souls is wrenching, chaotic work. This work returns us to our personal beginnings and our relationships to *mother* and *body* that we have inherited from generations of wounded women. We need to rediscover the matter (*mater*) from which we have come.

The following poem is by an unnamed woman struggling with reclamation and integration of her wounded Feminine in order that she may become more whole. In it we see what happens when Feminine energy turns against itself. We also see her longing to heal. It is called "She."

She
has lain forever,
coiled,
worm like,
at the bottom of my spine—sometimes in my gut.
A retrograde Kundalini.

She
of the tears,
of the sad face,
the vision redolent and weeping . . .
turned outward
from a venomous inward,
turned inward
from a repudiating outward.

She
lost in an abyss of confusion,
inhaling guilt,
embalmed in despair,
desolate,
helpless,
hopeless,
but hoping.

She
in me
but not me.
IN ME
BUT NOT ME.
In me . . . but not me . . .

She
venomous
and rageful,
jealous
and ravenous,
uncoiling,
slithering

into the light,
slinking surreptitiously, stealthily,
seeking succor,
sustenance,
support,
but re-coiling,
returning
to the refuge
of her hexed haunt
within.

She
yearns
to be re-membered.
To re-call
to re-play, her aching narrative.
To re-tell with anguish
the Hell
of tormented feelings,
of rejection smothering glimmers of longing
of rejections killing longing
of longing becoming rejection.

The
conflagration
between Me and She—symbiotic rivals—
is the challenge.

They,
when rivals no longer, but
independent—interdependent,
intertwining labyrinthine coils—
two voices
separate from each other
giving voice
giving ear
giving eye, to each other—
a helix of collateral support.

Only then,
can One,
be birthed. [6]

The Archetypal Feminine

The Feminine has appeared to us in many guises from time immemorial. Some images, such as Kuan Yin and the Madonna, encompass her in her gentle holding nature. In Sophia, we find wisdom. In Inanna, we find both compassion and fierceness (see Chapter 8). Durga, Kali, Baba Yaga, the Hag, and the Witch are names we have given to this Feminine power in her darker, seemingly destructive, and more ruthless aspects. If there is a Divine Feminine presence in the labyrinth, who is she? What is she calling us to do? What is this journey we undertake? Why do we dare it? What do we hope to accomplish? Are we learning what she wants us to learn?

The entrance to the labyrinth is traditionally in the west. The west, represented by the setting sun, connects us to the dark. In the Medicine Wheel I work with, it is in the position of Witch—she who lives in her body, in the earth, in the present moment, in her sensuality, with a knowledge of herbs, healing, and potions, and who transforms things from one state to another. When we enter the labyrinth and make our way toward the center, we are literally passing into and through the body of the Witch, being held by her, getting to know her, learning from her.

The journey to reconnect with our roots from thousands of years ago harks back to the Great Goddess in her cave. In doing so we recognize and experience what has been in the dark and longs to move into the light. She is calling out to us, urging us: Remember where you came from. Remember your roots. Remember your connection to the earth and the relentless, unremitting, never-ending process of birth and death, living and dying. She wants us to embrace the mystery of the unknown and the unfathomable, all that has been and is yet to be. She wants us to bear

6. Anonymous unpublished poem, 1992.

witness to the unfolding of creation in our universe and to the interconnectedness of each speck of life.

Her purpose is to help us become conscious. As we get to know the dark Feminine, we also get to know parts of ourselves that have lain in the shadow, sometimes connecting us to our personal histories, sometimes reaching back millennia into our ancestral or archetypal stories. In doing so, we open the mirror to our true nature and give it permission to be. Her intention is to unlock our hearts so we may live in a place of love and compassion. Our connection to the primordial energy of the Feminine gives us a different eye through which to see the world. She knows the complexity of the human condition and the paradoxical nature of life that holds both joy and anguish. She reminds us that in her cave both birth and death are inevitable and that is okay. It is the way life is. We are all born and we will all die. This is the ultimate mystery of existence and we are in its thrall.

When we are disconnected from this knowing we live in fear—of loving or being loved, of failure or success, of dearth or excess, of life, of others, of our inner demons, of pain. Fear causes us to close down and rein in, using our energies to protect ourselves rather than moving creatively forward into the world. It causes us to want to have power over others, believing that may give us a modicum of control over our own lives. But we are all in the same boat on the same planet, and each action will have a reaction that reverberates back to us in some form. The Feminine wants us to sink below fear into the unconditional love of the universe, to be able to know the anguish of the human condition because She is there holding us. When we no longer run in fear, but open our hearts, we cease to perpetrate harm on ourselves and others.

The Divine Feminine

Several years ago I had a profound experience of the Divine Feminine. I was with my women's group, which meets twice a year in California. This time, we met at a retreat center six miles north of the Mexican border. The terrain there is desert, with outcroppings of rock that form hills and caves. I awoke early the first morning, partly as a result of the three-hour time difference, and decided to dress and go for a walk. I saw a path leading through the grass and up a hill and followed it. (I later discovered this path was not as obvious as it appeared to me at that moment.) The path led me to a grassy area with rocky outcrops on both sides. I continued to wander slowly, taking in the landscape. Then, to my amazement I began to cry. This is not a usual event for me. I let the tears flow and continued around a particular outcrop on my left. On the ground I saw what looked like a stone bench. Bending down to get a closer look I turned my head. There, in an open-ended cave created by two great rocks, was the back of a statue of the Madonna. I was shocked. I went around to the front of the cave and kneeling on the earth, peered at her with tears streaming down my face. How could a mere white statue emanate such profound love and compassion? (I was raised Jewish, and therefore this encounter with the Madonna was even more unexpected.)

Shaking, I went down the hill to bring my friends back to see her. This time I lay on the earth at her feet, sobbing. I could feel her love, but moreso her compassion swirling around me and filling me. I felt held by the Divine Feminine presence in a way I never had before. I knew she was real, she existed, she was here for us. I have since felt her with me when I work with clients, when I lead workshops and retreats, as I am writing, and whenever I call upon her. It is her message that I want to communicate.

We do the most amazing things, often unconsciously, to bring that type of love and compassion into our lives. For many people (often beginning in childhood), the only time they have felt loved is when they have been ill. At these times others gathered around and the sick child (or adult) became the center of a whirlwind of loving and healing energy, feeding the souls of both giver and receiver. When the person recovered, the whirlwind ceased. Back to real life, the now-recovered person would become bereft, wanting more love and attention. The danger is that the person will create another illness in order to recapture what was lost—the love they received was not retained. It was not able to reach the deep loneliness and previous wounding, and to bathe their cells in love. Their programming didn't shift to *full* rather than *empty*. The healing journey that must now be taken is turning the eye of love back onto self, opening to the abundance of surrounding love—to the kind of love I felt from the Madonna. Ultimately it is love that heals. Truly opening our hearts to give and receive love brings peace.

Knowing the Feminine

The Madonna is one present-day manifestation of Goddess energy that has always been with us. The attempt to "virginalize" her has taken away her power and given women a chaste model of how they should behave. The appearance of the Black Madonna holds her polar opposite. Together they make a whole. They model the same light-and-dark split we find in so many women. Light-and-dark holds the mystery of how destruction, decay, and death lead to new growth, life, and creativity.

Not wanting to stay in the light-dark polarization, my women's group has been working with an energy we call the Red Madonna. She holds the energy of sexuality and earthiness and has a special blessing which I have introduced to others. The Red Madonna's libation is gin, the drink of Pelli the fire Goddess of Hawaii. It is poured into a red glass, and with great ceremony "spat" upon the one to be blessed. When the Red Madonna and her blessing are introduced, energy in a room changes dramatically. We fall into the hilarity of deep belly laughs, move out of our heads, and become grounded in the sensuality of our bodies. We are in her world where taboos (such as spitting) are broken. Both in blessing and in being blessed, her presence is palpable. Here she is:

The Red Madonna

I am hot, burning
in a clay cup,
scenting the air
with my wild fragrance,

soothing arms and backs,
stealing into minds

who have forgotten
where first they met me,

drenching the body
in desire,
letting it live
in the world, where
invisible moments connect
with longing,

impassioning
the eye
with sights
of yesterday
and tomorrow.

Possibility is now
A possibility.

Listen hard
for the processional.
Ready your tongue for
The entrance of joy.[7]
                    —*Dianne Joyce*

The Feminine Ignored

The Madonna wants to be known in her totality—in her White, Black, and Red manifestations. The Dark Feminine is *not* negative and destructive per se. When we ignore any aspect of her, block her energy, or run from the parts of ourselves that terrify us, she can get very angry and come through us in injurious ways. The Dark Feminine is not the Black Madonna. In this case, it is the Madonna in Her totality—Ignored. According to Carolyn Baker, "The dark Feminine (ignored), in both women and men, desires to capture,

---

7. Dianne Joyce, unpublished poem, 2000.

possess, confine, devour and feed off anything vital, alive, luscious and innocent—qualities so unlike itself"[8] (parentheses mine).

If we don't move toward life with our aliveness, we constellate forces inside us that don't want to let anyone else move toward that life either. We feed off others' lives, draining them of energy. This is the source of much of the negative-mother complex. It is a way women have developed to survive in controlling patriarchal structures. We cast negative, witchy spells on ourselves and each other in an attempt to stay safe, with the excuse of keeping others safe. One of the messages of the Hag as a representative of the dark Feminine is "Live until you die!" She certainly is not innocent *and* she is vital and alive. She knows death as an integral part of her aliveness. This is what the Hag wants of us. When we defy that dictum, she becomes very cranky in an attempt to get our attention and bring us back on the path.

Here is a dream depicting negative Feminine energy as it has been passed down through the generations. The dreamer, a woman in her fifties, was raised by a severely mentally ill mother who would go into rages. We could see her mother's madness as a manifestation of the Feminine ignored, that is, she did not allow her own life force to flow and therefore she felt she had to kill it in her daughter. Negative-mother complexes often show themselves in dreams in the form of spiders, in this case the most poisonous form, a black widow.

The dreamer has struggled all her life to free herself from this poison. In addition, she had recently been a passenger in a serious automobile accident from which she sustained severe injury to her right arm. At the time of the dream, she continued to struggle with considerable pain and physical limitation. Interestingly, her mother had lost complete use of *her* right arm after a falling accident in the home, for which she underwent several unsuccessful surgeries. At the time her mother was also in her early fifties, from which point on she gradually became an invalid until the time of her death twenty-five years later.

8. Carolyn Baker, *Reclaiming the Dark Feminine*, p. 37

In the dream I am a young woman in my twenties. I have returned to my childhood home and am sitting on the toilet in the upstairs bathroom. My mother is on my left. I look up and notice a large, fuzzy black spider in the upper right-hand corner of the ceiling. Somehow, I know it is meant for me. I am both horrified and fascinated. Sure enough, down it comes, landing on my right forearm. At first I am mesmerized, but soon begin to scream, "Get it off! Get it off!"

My father, who is now sitting on my mother's right, picks up a plastic kitchen spatula. "That's not going to kill anything!" I exclaim. Then my mother, using a metal spatula, swats the bug off my arm, but does not actually kill it. In a moment the spider reappears perched on my left shoulder and is looking up at me. I awaken and find myself pelting the bed with my pillow.

Upon bringing the dream to her session, the dreamer was very excited and immediately remarked upon the place where the spider had landed (her right arm). This was the site of her injury as well as her mother's. While she had enjoyed a far more positive relationship with her father, when it came down to protecting the children from his wife's wrath he was quite ineffectual. His behavior in the dream came as no surprise. The dreamer, however, felt good about her mother's actions. While the mother does knock the spider off, she doesn't kill it. That task is left to the daughter, who must complete the healing process herself.

In fact, both as a child and an adult, the dreamer's mother had also endured a turbulent and painful relationship with her own mother. In effect, both the dreamer and her mother had been un-mothered. We can see so clearly how this negative feminine energy has been passed down through the generations of women in this family.

Upon subsequent reflection, the dreamer came to realize that the "Dark Feminine" was a shared place, one both she and her mother had known. At the time of this writing, the dreamer has almost entirely recovered the use of her arm. She has also come into her own creativity, which in addition to offering its own rewards, has become, for her, a place of positive connection to both her mother and her grandmother.

While working with negative Feminine material during my analysis in Zurich the following poem popped out.

BETRAYAL

The word BETRAYAL reverberates relentlessly
On and on
like the hypnotic, frantic, drumbeat
of a
shamanic ritual.
BE TRAY A L !
BE TRAY A L !

I don't understand I cry out.
Who have I betrayed?
How have I betrayed you?

You have betrayed us it answers.
You have betrayed the covenant.

THE COVENANT!
What are you talking about?
What covenant?

And then there is silence.
Deathly, still, silence.
Worse than the accusation.
Worse,
because there is nothing to fight against or for . . .
just utter despair,
and so many tears.

The poem surprised me as I was not conscious of carrying this feeling around. As I pondered it, I realized my attempts to free myself from the strictures that bound me for most of my life were so difficult because on a cellular level I was breaking an ancient covenant that carried the following edicts: I must not be fully alive. I must not step forward into my creativity. I must not have a life of passion. I must not feel joy. I most definitely must not show myself or succeed. I must be hidden, quiet, and acquiescent. Then I would be safe. Whenever I would step out, I felt horrible guilt and shame. Finding the feelings intolerable and not understanding why, I would retreat back into my safe but sad and depressing cave.

In conversations with many women, including my clients, I see so clearly that this is not just *my* story. It is many women's stories. How often have we broken these strictures in ungrounded and frenzied ways. How much have our addictions, promiscuity, rage, vengefulness, and our power drives been attempts to break free of these unconsciously imposed restrictions? We have raged against men as the enemy, when the enemy is also within. Becoming conscious of the "covenant" and the witchy spells we cast on ourselves and others is an essential first step in unlocking the door of the cage in which we have been trapped.

Finding Our Voices

For many women speaking the truth of what we feel and know has been terrifying. In these troubling times, it has moved me deeply, to hear the voices of so many women raised strongly and clearly for all to hear. The creativity that has come from these women, as we together have faced formidable odds, is impressive. It has been the voice of the Feminine speaking out for life, having compassion for all, and struggling to be heard in a world that is still run by power over others rather than power from within. I have great hope as this energy builds, that something profound will change on our planet. Melinda Burns captures the essence of finding our voices in this poem.

She Spoke

She spoke
where she would not have
spoken before, but
excused, found reason for silence.

She spoke
where she would have tried

smiling before, and
pushed her pain to the corners.

She spoke
where she would not have
dared before,
exploded the world as they knew it.

She did not speak loudly
she was not hysterical
she uttered no threats
though a threat rang round her.

She spoke
and conjured the precipice,
a woman pushed to the edge
and knowing her wings.[9]

—*Melinda Burns*

The following dream emerged for one woman as she found herself struggling with having been silenced (by others and herself) and her longing to find her own voice: "I have been given several harmonicas. They either belonged to Martin Luther King or they were used at his funeral. Then someone pulls out a dusty old flute that is mine and gives it to me."

Martin Luther King's story had been an inspiration in this woman's life. She had been terrified of speaking out. Martin Luther King was killed for speaking out, and this dream affirmed her own fears. However, she was given her own flute, her own voice that had not been used in a long time. (She actually does have a flute which she had not played for years.) The dream was a message from her unconscious that it was time to let go of the harmonica, which did not belong to her, and to pick up the flute, which does.

How often do we abandon ourselves to be abused by others because we follow a set of rules that are imposed from outside, not from within? We do so each time we do not speak up for ourselves

9. Melinda Burns, unpublished poem, 2001.

or others. We give the message to our wounded parts that we are not there for them. We are abandoning ourselves! If we can't protect ourselves, who can? We allow ourselves to be abused because we are afraid of seeming "not nice." The following story offers some understanding of how this may have developed in us.

Several years ago, a friend shared with me this incident concerning her eight-year-old daughter, Sarah. That morning in school, Sarah had gone to the washroom with her friend Dina. There, on the washroom wall, was a graffiti saying *Dina Loves Danny!* Both girls were incensed. How could anyone do this! It was not true! It was not fair! They went back to the classroom and Sarah couldn't bear the humiliation to her friend Dina. She returned to the washroom and later reported, "Mama, I went there intending to rub it off but instead found myself writing on the wall, "How dare you." How dare you! What a profound statement! What happened to the how-dare-yous in our lives? How many how-dare-yous have we stifled? How many of us have experienced what Sarah did? When this writing was discovered by a teacher and Sarah admitted her guilt, she was severely reprimanded. Instead of being acknowledged for speaking a truth, albeit in a not very appropriate manner, Sarah was made to feel less than human for writing on the wall. Sarah said, "Mama, they made me feel like I had exploded the world!" Sarah's how-dare-you is the response from the dark Feminine layer of ourselves, and her teacher's response shows how the eight-year-old in all of us has been taught to shut up. All of us have learned that speaking out can get us into trouble. We learn that it is better to stay quiet.

As women age, more of this powerful Feminine energy seems to come through. I have observed this in both myself and many of my women friends who are in their fifties, sixties, and seventies. We are no longer so polite or accepting of others' behaviors. If we don't like it, we say so. A friend told me the following story. She had just parked her car in the back alley of her home and saw a van idling a few feet away. To her amazement, a man got out of the passenger seat, opened the rear of the van, and threw trash onto the street. Without hesitating, she went up to his window and in a no-nonsense voice told him to pick it up immediately

Trembling, the man put some of the trash back into his van, but not all of it, and ran back to his seat. She again knocked on the window indicating there was more. The procedure repeated itself. This time, only one piece of trash was left. She picked it up, knocked on his window a third time, and threw it in. To preclude his coming back to take revenge she stood behind the van where he could see her and stared at the car, as if memorizing the license plate. She felt so proud of herself. This is an example of fierce energy speaking through us. The more we take a stand in such daily occurrences, the more the energy is primed and flows naturally.

The Feminine and Sorrow

As I prepared to walk the labyrinth one day I was thinking about the issue of sorrow. The question came to me: Does all wounding relate to the Feminine? Following the twists and turns as I pondered, it became very clear that the answer was a resounding *Yes*. The Feminine is about relationship, the relationship we have with our physical bodies, with our emotional and inner lives, and with Spirit. It is also about relationship to another—friend, family, city, country, pets, plants. Most wounding happens when there is discord between self and any of the above. This discord can reinforce some of the negative conditioning we carry with us. It can confirm our thinking that we really are unlovable. The most intense pain we suffer is from feeling abandoned and unloved, and the most profound aspect is when we have abandoned ourselves on either a human or a spiritual level.

How do we reconcile this with the pain and suffering that confronts us daily? With television and the Internet, visual images of human agony abound. If we open ourselves even a little bit to it, we feel swamped and helpless. The more we bury it, the more we detach and become silent. Witness the following poem by Lois Zachariah.

Falling

She is vertiginous
while children die.
She tumbles over and over

and many are hungry.
She is whirling down in the acrid dark
even as the wanderers come in to eat.

For several weeks she dreams that she is falling.
She falls down and up.
She moves through sediments
of past graces and desolations, recalling
the cloud of unknowing,
the wide rents in the Spirit.

For several years she knows that she is falling.
She falls asleep in the light,
in the dark, in the mind,
in the recesses of the Soul,
that Spirit thing, trawling
in deep water for light,
the slightest shadow of light.

She sleeps, she falls asleep,
remembering the photo
of the small children
who do not smile,
who are falling also
into that knowledge
for which there are no words,
only growls of suffering.

Still she falls, into the crevice,
then into the vacuum,
then into the dread.
She despairs, is breathless
in the place where breathing ceases.

She is drowning even as we speak.
She hears a litany which reeks
of others' fears, she hears

the impossible clichés of
entitlement.

She drives to work and thinks
happy thoughts of her death
while many die who want to live.
What is she, and we, dear
reader, to make of this?

Where is the balance in the world?
There are 1000 hierarchies of suffering
which no God of mercy sees.
Earth hums with prayers which are hurled
back, bouncing off Your Shield.[10]

   —*Lois Zachariah*

The anguish of the human condition is impossible to hold without divine help, and without a community of intrepid and compassionate others who join with us. It is too much to bear alone.
In the wake of September 11th and its repercussions, we know
this only too well. I am deeply moved by stories I hear from
around the world, where people are being victimized and others
step in, risking their own lives, to give those in need support in
whatever way is necessary.

   In Zachariah's poem we feel her despair as she experiences suffering on the planet as an indication we have been abandoned by
God. Abandonment by God is one of the most devastating experiences and perhaps the most profound pain we can feel. Often,
other abandonments spiral around to the feeling—if there really
were a God how could he let this happen to me? I remember my
river experience where I sobbed with grief and raged at the inequities in life. Since meeting the Madonna in her cave, I feel differently and have a deepened understanding of life's journey in
both its complexity and simplicity. I have become immersed in the
mystery of the larger story and feel the Madonna's compassion for

---

10. Lois Zachariah, Unpublished poem, 1997.

all life. It doesn't take the pain away, for we live with that always. As we open our hearts to her love, we open to the abundance of love in the universe, flowing through us toward ourselves and others. In the words of Jennifer Paine Welwood:

The Dakini Speaks

My friends, let's grow up.
Let's stop pretending we don't know the deal here.
Or if we truly haven't noticed, let's wake up and notice.
Look: Everything that can be lost, will be lost.
It's simple—how could we have missed it for so long?
Let's grieve our losses fully, like ripe human beings,
But please, let's not be so shocked by them.
Let's not act so betrayed,
As though life had broken her secret promise to us.
Impermanence is life's only promise to us,
And she keeps it with ruthless impeccability.
To a child she seems cruel, but she is only wild,
And her compassion exquisitely precise:
Brilliantly penetrating, luminous with truth,
She strips away the unreal to show us the real.
This is the true ride—let's give ourselves to it!
Let's stop making deals for safe passage:
There isn't one anyway, and the cost is too high.
We are not children anymore.
The true human adult gives everything for what
Cannot be lost.
Let's dance the wild dance of no hope![11]

As reported in China Galland's *The Bond Between Women*, many women and men who have survived unbelievable horrors or who have witnessed the unbearable and have borne it, develop a fierce compassion that flows toward others. (See China Galland's *The Bond Between Women: A Journey to Fierce Compassion* for some striking examples.) Their phenomenal courage speaks to us

11. Jennifer Paine Welwood, *Poems for the Path*, 1998, 1999, p. 15.

and demonstrates that we can carry on. They have dealt with the unimaginable, survived, and have a wisdom born of their endurance. They have not run from it, nor shut it off through drink or drugs. By being in it and with it they allow the pain to flow through their bodies. It never leaves totally, but its presence becomes a reminder of the sanctity and fragility of the gift of life. It is a prod to reach out to others in pain, to confront evil and negligence when it appears. The stories of such people are everywhere. A father whose son was killed in an industrial accident spends his time educating young people about safety on the job site. A woman whose daughter was murdered collects money for others in her situation so that they can get some time away to heal.

Connecting with this truth gives us power to be in the world with Fierce Compassion. We can only do this by not running from the pain and staying awake. When life is being threatened, we allow ourselves to feel our rage and become energized to take steps to ameliorate what we see. We become less afraid to let the fierceness show and stand our ground.

Understanding the Dark

Because we confuse the dark with evil, it is important to differentiate between the two. Jung described that which was as yet unseen and unknown as in the shadow, or in the dark. We have both a personal shadow and a collective shadow. Our personal shadow contains hidden talents as well darker emotions such as rage, jealousy, hatred, judgment, guilt, remorse, and destructive and harmful things we may have done to others and ourselves. Collective shadow is comprised of unconscious elements shared with our extended family, city, nation, and planet as a whole. One example of collective shadow is the shameful way residents of most countries have treated indigenous peoples who were there before them.

Evil, on the other hand, is against life, completely disconnected from Feminine grounding. It has no compassion, no humanity, no remorse. It is for itself and its own power. Evil is fed by Ego needs. It will do *anything* to maintain that sense of power even if it involves killing other life forms. Timothy McVeigh blew up the government buildings in Oklahoma City and referred to his victims as "collateral damage." In the same way the wounded and dying citizens of Iraq have been called collateral damage.

Were the September 11th terrorists evil? What differentiates them from McVeigh is that they sacrificed themselves in the process. These men come from a society where women are subjugated and the Feminine deplored. As a result they are disconnected from any feminine influence, leaving them open to a religious fervor so great they would give up their own lives in search of glory in the afterlife. It is hard to believe there is a God who would condone such acts.

Much has been written on evil from philosophical, psychological, and religious perspectives. In an attempt to understand it, we have created many theories but no one really knows why certain people are capable of committing atrocious acts without feeling remorse. They frequently justify their actions with bizarrely rational thinking and are often charismatic enough to brainwash others into following suit.

Starting a war is about wielding power. Killing in war is about dehumanizing the enemy by filling people's minds with propaganda and blatant lies to serve the power needs of the few at the top. Mass genocide has become common. This is evil. Horrible things happen in our world in the name of progress. There is short-sightedness born of greed. As long as we get what we need, it doesn't matter if we are poisoning the planet and depleting its resources. The future is now; that is all that counts. We want profits and progress. If you attempt to challenge this view you're told that you are soft, leftist, naive, living in a dream world. You are told to "get real." That is what we desperately need to do. We need to *get real!*

Working with personal shadow is vital. Having a shadow and shadow-type feelings are all a part of the human condition. It is normal. We get into difficulty with our shadow in two ways. If we don't become conscious of shadow feelings, we tend to act them out. Acting them out can have horrific consequences for all concerned. Rather than being run by our feelings, we need to feel them, name them, and then choose our course of action.

Here's a simple example. I have a wonderful little dog called Muffin who has been a great teacher for me. She is intelligent and playful, loving and funny, but she has one "fault." She has a shrill bark that comes out of nowhere and makes my whole body jump. There are times when these barks come one after another to the point where I can feel myself going into a rage. I want to shut her up and the images that come to me are sometimes quite awful. Although I don't act on them, adrenaline pumps through my body and I have to make a conscious decision to desist. At that point, I breathe and wonder why I am so on edge. All of this has made me profoundly compassionate for people who reach their limit and react. Although I in no way condone violence against another, I appreciate the struggle involved in controlling such impulses.

By daring to imagine ourselves committing acts our rational minds abhor, we can keep those acts on an imaginal level. It gives an outlet for anger without our having to act it out. Erishkigal, who is the shadow side of the Goddess Inanna, represents those parts in us. In Chapter 9 you can read about a woman who allowed herself to connect with her inner Erishkigal and to put her images down on paper. If we can't allow ourselves to imagine, we are forever cut off from our compassion for others and are left with judgment. Judgments don't heal, they merely deepen the divide within and cut us off from our essential nature even more.

The second way shadow gets us into trouble is when we identify as the "bad" one. Once we do that, we can end up in a downward spiral of self-recrimination from which we feel there is no escape. This can lead to destructive behavior both to ourselves and others. A woman in her forties had the following dream which embarked her on a process of looking at her personal shadow.

It is a story about a young boy who is evil. I was trying to fly. It took great effort, and each time it didn't last very long. Someone was telling me about seeing this boy. He lived with his mother. We met him later, when he was in his teens. The last time I went to fly I had to go by myself. I was still trying to fly through flat, pastoral countryside. I was afraid and hoped I wouldn't see him. His mother told me he either was now, or had been, engaged to be married. I wondered who would marry someone like him. I was surprised to learn he was now in his mid-twenties. When I did meet up with him, he was doing some sort of outdoor work. He was telling me, or I was being told, of some of the evil things he was doing and had done. I was afraid. He's maturing?

This woman has been struggling for years to put behind her a period in her life when she acted in ways not in sync with how she wanted to see herself. During that time she had been depressed and angry, and had taken out her feelings on other people, leaving her feeling remorse and guilt. As a consequence, she has grappled all her life with feelings that she was inferior and an inherently bad (evil) person. In this dream, we can see how she has been trying, with great difficulty, to fly above it all. The dream ends with fear as the negative Masculine energy inside seems to be maturing. As we began working with these dark parts of herself in analysis, she came to see that she was not evil, but someone who had been in a great deal of pain. As we explored the source of her pain, her compassion and love for the wounded parts of herself and others grew. She no longer feared this "evil" young man who also began to change.

More Dreams of the Feminine

Here is a small sampling of the dreams of several women to show how the Feminine is currently appearing to them. The first two are from the same woman. They give a sense of how the unconscious portrays the wounded Feminine, and how that image shifts as healing proceeds. The dreamer, a sixty-year-old woman, has spent most of her life separated from her inner Feminine self. In the first dream, she is taking a break from work (her outside life), but is too frantic to enjoy it. The Feminine in this dream is very ill and almost comatose.

I am at work. I take off at lunchtime, with my son and an unknown woman. We go to the farm. I look out the window and see a car racing towards me but they slam the brakes on. The car is filled with young men and women. They all come into the house. I am upset. I must get back to my job. My God, I will be late. They brought a huge pile of laundry. I can hear the washer going. I go look, thinking they are using my old wringer washer but no, they have brought a new, small automatic one. I have to go to the bathroom. There is a sick woman lying on the floor. She must give herself blood transfusions. I can see a little pool of blood and an empty plastic blood bag lying on the floor. I have to step over all this to get to the toilet. I am so upset. I tell my son to get them out of here; we have to go. What am I to do? I could phone work and say we got into an accident or a traffic jam but I am somehow not sure. We get back to the office and there is no big problem about our being late.

She goes to the farm in the country, a place of the Feminine. A car full of young people threatens to invade her, and does. She is trying to get them out, turn things back to the way they were. She goes in the bathroom, a place of "expression," and there she finds this very wounded part of herself needing lifeblood. She has to step over the woman rather than connecting with her to see if she might be able to help. The dreamer was quite disturbed by the graphic images in this dream. The second dream came several months later and indicates she is now feeling safe enough to explore what the Feminine might mean to her.

I am at some kind of institution where women are treated for mental problems. I do not live in but others do. I see one very thin, flat-chested woman in my group. She is beginning to speak up. I am very interested. Now there will be some kind of interaction. I see families sitting with women who they are visiting.

Here the dreamer has become interested in this "thin, flat-chested woman," one who does not yet look like a woman but is beginning to speak up. With this interest, the healing process can begin. Her attitude has changed from the first dream where the

Feminine is ignored, to this dream where the dreamer begins to pay attention.

The following is the dream of a woman in her fifties in the process of waking up to how she betrayed herself throughout life. She has followed dictums set down by an authority she has always unconsciously obeyed without question, and in the process has denied her inner authority. This dream has come as she is changing careers and looking more deeply into her patterns of behavior in relationships.

> I am standing outside a huge store like a Costco. I don't really want to go in. I am frightened but I follow someone inside. It is huge with great empty spaces and I am frightened. You have to buy a minimum of two kilograms of food and I don't want to buy that much. I see my daughter and she asks me to cut some flesh off her back around her left shoulder. She is insistent. I don't want to do it but find myself doing it anyway. There is no blood and at first she has no reaction. Then she begins to feel faint. Two very old women are watching this process and nodding their heads as if they understood what was going on. I am very upset. The scene changes and I am at an event and seem to be looking after all these children. No one pays any attention to me and no one else is looking after them. I am in a panic and feel like I don't belong. All I want is some contact with someone.

This is a fascinating dream for it depicts how women have given a "pound of flesh" quite unconsciously to maintain the status quo. The dreamer enters a vast building with many empty spaces and rules having to do with gluttony and greed—a grim depiction of the underbelly of our society. When bloodless surgical procedures occur in dreams, they indicate that this is a ritual event. As the old women look on, nodding in a knowing way, we see how the expected excision has gone on through the generations. The daughter, representing the part of the dreamer that is still maturing, shows signs that she is being affected. The dreamer is very upset and begins to question everything she has done. In the last part of the dream, we get a clear portrayal of how the dreamer has served others to the exclusion of herself and her growing consciousness that this is no longer viable. What she wants is real connection, which is not available to her if she sticks to old modes of being. The transition process is a very painful one for her.

The next two dreams give glimpses of how the power of the Feminine comes to us. The first dreamer inherits a ring from her grandmother; the second dreamer has an encounter with a goddess figure. In both instances the unknown women represent Self figures who carry the dreamers' inner Spiritual wisdom.

> I was sitting in a semi-dark room. I know I was with another person, I think an older woman, but I could not see her. I only felt her presence. In front of me there was a brown paper box full of jewelry. The things were all mixed up so it was difficult to see them clearly. A bright yellow light shone on the box, making it the only thing visible in the room. The woman picked up a ring and showed it to me. It was valuable and very beautiful. It was round and gold and on top of it was a square filled with lines of diamonds and onyx. There were four lines and four rows of stones, and the onyx was either at the beginning or at the end of the row. It was so beautiful I marveled at it and said I would like very much to have it. I knew this was the ring I had been looking for, for a long time. While looking at the ring I remembered that after my grandmother died, I had inherited one of her rings. I then realized I was wearing it on my left hand, but had forgot all about it. It looked similar to the one in the box but it had diamonds and my sapphire birthstone also in lines but arranged diagonally. There were two differences in the rings. My grandmother's ring had an oval shape instead of being square, and my grandmother's ring was used and the one I found in the box looked brand new. I felt very deeply moved by this gift, and thought I was very fortunate.

Because of its round, closed shape a ring symbolizes continuity and wholeness. The dreamer, a woman in her fifties, had immigrated to Canada from another country years ago. As a result she has felt disconnected from her roots, particularly the gifts of the

line of women from which she has come. She is presented with a
new ring by this unknown, wise part of herself. Once she discov-
ers the new ring, it becomes apparent to her that she has had this
wisdom all along, only forgotten about it. Now, she can unite her
newly found treasure with the one she has carried with her, and
move forward in her life in a more whole way. This was a pivotal
dream in her healing process.

This fifty-year-old dreamer meets a representative of the goddess. Being held in love and compassion by this goddess figure allows the dreamer to ask for forgiveness and move on in her life.

> I am with a woman in India. I don't know who she is. She is
> taking me to a shrine located in a restaurant. We pass through
> many rooms in this restaurant; all are dirty and crowded. The
> dust and the dirt repulse me. We enter a large, rectangular room
> with hardwood floors, wood panelling on the walls, and a low
> wooden ceiling. There is a fireplace with a black iron grate. My
> guide goes over to the fireplace and lights a candle on the floor.
> She nods to our right. I turn and see a woman sitting on the
> floor, cross-legged and meditating. I go over and sit in front of
> her. She looks at me, deeply, with kind eyes. I realize we can
> communicate without speech, and we are telepathic. I "tell" her
> she looks like one of my husband's relatives, Anna. She smiles
> and asks me how I am related to Anna. I tell her she is very
> beautiful. She continues to smile and nod in my direction. Now
> her appearance changes. Her face becomes more remote. Her
> hair is now a light brown and her eyes are blue. Her appearance
> has been transformed. I start to weep uncontrollably with great
> sobs. She puts her arms around me and I cry, from the bottom
> of my heart, "I need forgiveness." She continues to hold and
> comfort me, and then takes my left hand in hers. I pull my hand
> away, but she is insistent. I give her my left hand, palm up. She
> places my hand in a fold in her abdomen, which is soft, as if she
> has just had a baby. She then makes a strange, humping move-
> ment with her abdomen so that it is pressed down on my hand.
> She does this several times (I think three but I'm not sure). I
> wake up.

Notice how sensual the connection is as the goddess figure in this dream insists upon intimate physical contact. Although the dreamer initially resists, it is through the body that healing happens. The dreamer was deeply moved and felt she was coming home to herself and her connection to a feminine spiritual presence in her life in a way she never had before.

The following was dreamt by a sixty-year-old woman who was at a turning point in her creative life. She is about to move on from a functional and goal-oriented way of being to one more based on a Feminine aesthetic.

> I appear to be ready to vacate a building made of thick gray cement that is functional rather than aesthetic. The caretaker tells me that our contract will end after I clean one of the toilet stalls in a large basement public washroom.
>
> I go to the basement to see the toilet stall. On the left side of the toilet there is a large cardboard box with its back right corner filled with mounds of drying feces. I get nauseous at the sight and at the thought of having to clean it. I leave the washroom and walk across a large corridor to a counter that faces the washroom. I hope to finalize my contract with the woman behind the counter.
>
> The woman tells me not to write any more mono myths. When I ask her why she says "it gets too confusing for people who have already gone through the journey." After she says this I become filled with energy go back into the washroom, put on rubber gloves, take a brush to the toilet, empty the box of feces into the toilet, spray and disinfect the stall, write and leave a note that says, "Do not Flush for . . . hours so the feces have time to break up and not clog the toilet."

This woman has been blocked in her creative expression. Her inner caretaker informs her she will be free once she cleans out a toilet stall in a large basement public washroom. Since it is a public washroom, not the one in her home, it indicates that the block comes from the societal or collective part of her. Her association to mono myth was the Hero's journey. She felt she had to meet criteria dissociated from her feminine nature, and by expressing herself as she really wanted to, she would meet disdain in the outside world. She was aware of the dictum to conquer her demons rather than engage with them in a creative way. Once given permission to try a different way by the part of herself represented by the woman behind the counter, she is suddenly filled with a new kind of energy. She is able to clean out residue in her psyche, and move forward in a new way. This is the ever present challenge for all of us who wish to push the boundaries of the familiar and the acceptable and express a knowing from within.

In the 1930s, Jung gave a series of seminars based on the visions of a young American woman named Christiana Morgan. Jung was the first to differentiate between Masculine and Feminine energies, and was able to open many women to a part of themselves that had lain dormant up until then. But Jung was both a man and a product of his time, and was not able to allow the process to unfold as much as it might have. In her introduction to a reprinting of these seminars, Claire Douglas, an American Jungian Analyst, writes:

> Christiana Morgan's active imaginations grew to be a series of over one hundred fantasies that led her though a personal but also archetypal Feminine rite of initiation. Through her visions, Morgan confronted unexpected ideas about women, a Feminine imaginal world including women's mystery rites and impressions of herself as an assertive and active Feminine heroine. Morgan may have been the first woman to journey thus on an inward heroic quest that engaged the darkly potent side of women's psychology. Many other images offer a view of women's psychological development that is only now becoming generally recognised. In 1926 it was not one for which either Morgan or Jung seemed quite ready.[12]

We are pioneers. Never before in human history have women had the opportunity, courage, support, and the irrefutable necessity to live from those places in themselves that connect with this

---

12. Claire Douglas, *Visions,* introduction.

deepest wisdom and truth. In a sense, Jung started us out. He saw where we had to go, but we are moving into and beyond ourselves in ways he didn't imagine. We are finding our power from within and learning to give voice to that power in the world. We are learning to overcome our fears and speak out what we know. Never before was this so important as now.

> The manner and appearance of a prophet,
> our secret origins, these are born
> of a woman who still lives inside us,
> though she's hiding from what we've become.[13]
>
> —*Rumi*

---

13. John Moyne and Coleman Barks, *Unseen Rain: Quatrains of Rumi*, p. 8.

PART III:

Myths and Fairy Tales of the Journey

OVERVIEW
CHAPTER SIX: Theseus and the Minotaur
CHAPTER SEVEN: Demeter and Persephone
CHAPTER EIGHT: Inanna
CHAPTER NINE: Vassilisa the Beautiful

OVERVIEW

Thus far we have explored many dimensions of the labyrinth and the Feminine, and their relationship to each other. In this section we will deepen our understanding by moving into the archetypal realm. Archetypal stories come to us in the form of both myths and fairy tales. They give us a sense of the larger patterns that underlie our present-day human stories. In each case I discuss there is a journey to a center, and in two of the myths the journey is repeated yearly. Once we know our way, we can undertake the journey when necessary, experience what is needed and return renewed.

We will begin with the Theseus story, a perfect example of the Hero's journey. In it we have a Hero who traverses the labyrinth to meet, in the form of the Minotaur, that which is unknown and hidden in himself. Instead of engaging with this power in some way, however, Theseus kills it and in doing so misses an opportunity for transformation.

In the Demeter and Persephone myth, we are given a sense of the underlying pattern when one is raped into the underworld rather than choosing to descend consciously. Although we do not have a labyrinth per se in this story, the journey is labyrinthine and a powerful teacher of what happens under these circumstances.

The Myth of the Sumerian Goddess Inanna is an example of a chosen feminine descent to the underworld. We learn from her careful preparation, her slow descent, her time in the underworld, and her eventual release. She is transformed in the process, and returns with renewed strength and courage.

In the fairy tale of Vassilisa the Beautiful, we experience both the negative mother and the dark Feminine. Here we learn what we must do in order to protect ourselves, survive the experience, and grow.

The Dishonored Minotaur, by Friedrich Durrenmatt
(1921–1990).

6

THESEUS AND THE MINOTAUR

We can't ask
for what we know we want:
we have to ask to be led
someplace we never dreamed of going,
a place we don't want to be.

We'll find ourselves there
one morning,
opened like leaves,
and it will be all right.[1]

—Kathleen Norris

The myth of Theseus meeting the Minotaur in the center of the labyrinth is a classical Hero myth. It is an example of the old, heroic, might-over-matter approach that not only neglects but also abuses the Feminine. There is no death and rebirth; there is only

---

1. Kathleen Norris, excerpted from "Answered Prayers," in *Claiming the Spirit Within: A Sourcebook of Women's Poetry*, p. 160.

death. This is typical of the attitude of our times, which has worshipped the Hero as the ideal. Theseus' "descent" to the center of the labyrinth, was where he could connect with his shadow and reunite with the goddess energy that had been so powerful but was slowly being replaced by the growing strength of patriarchy. It does not happen for him.

The Theseus Story

Theseus was born of two fathers, King Aigeus of Athens, a mortal, and Poseidon, God of the Sea. His human father left a sword and sandals under a rock with instructions that when Theseus was strong enough to lift the rock and retrieve the items, he was to come to find him in Athens. Theseus accomplished the feat at age sixteen, and arrived in Athens already a hero for having vanquished monsters and tyrants along the way.

Characters in the Myth of Theseus

Theseus . . . . The Hero
King Aigeus . . . . . King of Athens, Theseus' human father
Poseidon . . . . God of the Sea, Theseus' nonhuman father
King Minos . . . . . King of Crete
Queen Pasiphae . . Wife of King Minos
Ariadne . . . . Minos' daughter
Phaedra . . . . Minos' daughter, wife of Theseus
Hypolytus . . . . . . Phaedra and Theseus' son
Daedelus . . . . Master craftsman and creator of the labyrinth
Minotaur . . . . Offspring of White Bull and Queen Pasiphae

King Aigeus took Theseus as his heir amid public rejoicing. Medea, King Aigeus' consort, attempts to poison Theseus in order to ensure her own son's ascent to the throne. Her plot is thwarted. Soon after, the city is plunged into mourning by the arrival from Crete of the tribute-vessel. It had come for the boys and girls sent off to be devoured by the Minotaur, as a blood debt for the loss of King Minos' son and heir at the hands of the Athenians.

Who is the Minotaur and where did he come from? The story is as follows. King Minos of Crete prayed to Poseidon, asking him for a magnificent bull worthy of being sacrificed in Poseidon's honor. When the bull arrived King Minos found it so wondrous he was not able to sacrifice it, and sacrificed another bull instead. If one makes a vow to the Gods, one cannot defy them. Poseidon was furious. In order to mete out punishment, Poseidon called upon Aphrodite, the Goddess of Love. She caused Queen Pasiphae, King Minos' wife, to lust after the bull. In order to consummate her passion, Queen Pasiphae had Daedelus, the mastercraftsman, create a hollow wooden cow for her, into which she climbed. Their offspring was the Minotaur, a being with a man's body and a bull's head, who fed on human flesh. In order to conceal his shame, King Minos had an impenetrable labyrinth made by Daedelus, and in its heart he placed the Minotaur.

The required quota to be sent to Crete was seven youths and seven maidens. Among these went Theseus; according to most versions, by his own choice, though others say by lot. At his departure, his father asked him to change the black sail of the sacrificial ship to a white one, should Theseus return alive.

On his arrival on Crete, King Minos mocked Theseus' claim to be the son of Poseidon, and challenged him to retrieve a ring which he (Minos) threw into the sea. Theseus dove into the water and received from the sea-nymphs not only the ring, but also a golden crown. His exploit caused King Minos' daughter, Ariadne, to fall in love with him. Inspired to save Theseus' life, Ariadne consulted with Daedelus who instructed her to secretly give Theseus a ball of thread with which he could retrace his steps through the labyrinth, and a sword with which to kill the Minotaur.

Theseus was successful and fled with Ariadne to the Island of Naxos, where he abandoned her and then sailed back to Athens. There Ariadne was met by Dionysus, the god of spirit and passion, and she joined with him. In spite of Theseus' agreement with his father to change the ship's flag from black to white if he survived, Theseus "forgot." His father, unable to bear his grief, jumped into the sea and drowned.

The Wisdom in the Myth

Theseus, the hero, with the help of Ariadne (Feminine, anima, sometimes also referred to as the Great Goddess and as Persephone, Queen of the Underworld), succeeds in killing a threatening aspect (the Minotaur), by traversing the labyrinth. This is symbolically a descent into the underworld, the domain of the Great Mother where transformation can occur, but Theseus' attitude toward the Feminine is not changed as a result of his experience. Although he is a powerful leader of men, his treatment of the Feminine and his understanding of Eros (relationships) deteriorates after he kills the Minotaur. We see this, among other things, in his abandonment of Ariadne and his "forgetting" to change the flag, resulting in his father's death.

Theseus is the Hero. His mother was a princess and he had two fathers. His human father, King Aigeus, was childless (no growth potential), except for Theseus. We know from the stories about him that he had been in discord with the Goddess Aphrodite. Since Aphrodite represents love and eros (the Feminine), this would indicate a difficulty in King Aigeus' relationship to the Feminine. This is confirmed by his choice of consort, Medea the witch, who attempted to poison Theseus when he arrived in Athens. What King Aigeus offered Theseus is a human model of a hero who shows physical strength and vanquishes his enemies.

The second father of Theseus is the God Poseidon. In the Greek pantheon, Poseidon, Zeus, and Hades are the three sons of Kronos. The kingdom was divided between them. Poseidon became the God of the Seas and water in general. If we take the symbolic interpretation of water as representing the unconscious and the emotions, then Poseidon's realm of water is the intermediary between Zeus as god of the upper world (light), and Hades as god of the underworld (dark). As the father of Theseus, Poseidon offered him the watery, emotional, unconscious elements that seemed to be missing from his human father Aigeus.

As true of heroic men then and now, Theseus set out for adventure and put himself in positions where he met and overcame powerful challenges, and therefore proved his masculinity. His arrival in Athens and reunification with his father is triumphant, made even more dramatic by his escape from death at the hands of Medea. Soon after, Theseus is either chosen, or chooses, to sail to Crete as a part of the debt paid to King Minos for the death of King Minos' son and heir.

Let's change focus for the moment and turn to King Minos, his wife, Pasiphae, and Crete. Legend has it that King Minos was the son of Europa and Zeus (conceived while Zeus was in the form of a white bull), and was brought up by King Asterion. He has the reputation of being a wise and fair ruler.

Pasiphae, his wife, was the daughter of the Sun God Helios and her mother was a descendent of the Moon Goddess, Perseis. She was the sister of both Circe (one of the goddesses who initiated Odysseus into the world of the Feminine) and Medea (the witch consort who tried to kill Theseus). Her connection to the moon (*luna*) suggests lunacy, which was certainly the state that possessed her when she mated with the white bull.

Why did King Minos, with all his wisdom, fail to sacrifice the white bull he had been given by Poseidon? Was this King Minos' disconnection from the watery depths of the unconscious? Was it a rebellion, an attempt at autonomy? It raised the ire of both Poseidon and Aphrodite. Aphrodite was known to have been born on the crest of a wave. She comes naturally from Poseidon's realm. She was angered at the slight, but why is it then that Queen Pasiphae must pay for King Minos' misdeed? Why did Aphrodite do it in such a humiliating manner? Perhaps King Minos' neglect of the Feminine (Aphrodite and Queen Pasiphae) infuriated them, and raised in the Queen a longing to be rejoined with that from which she had been separated. The bull, a gift from the God of the Sea, symbolized raw power of the unconscious and emotional depths. This is a warning that the unconscious or the Feminine can't be ignored.

Pasiphae's union with the bull was curious. It was assisted by Daedelus, the master craftsman who was also responsible for the construction of the labyrinth that housed the resultant Minotaur. The Minotaur produced by this union had a man's body and a bull's head and lived only on human flesh. He was a monster created by the union of the wounded Feminine (Pasiphae) with the depths of the unconscious (Poseidon). There is much to be learned here. If someone is bull-headed, is he not stubborn? Wouldn't stubbornness describe an aspect of a patriarchal culture that wants to cling to its old powers and not change? The Minotaur is the union of unmitigated passion with power. How often has patriarchal culture led with brute physical strength and thrusting sexuality, while its decision making and destructiveness have been as clumsy and unconscious as a bull's. This bull-headed man destroys human beings. His unconscious, repressed, and locked-away terror has been devouring human potential and creativity for centuries. King Minos was wise to put the Minotaur into a sealed place for he knew something very dangerous was unleashed when he defied Poseidon.

That the Minotaur was held in the womb of the Great Mother—the center of the labyrinth—is also fascinating. He, created from rage and passion, became a part of her power that cannot be set loose into the world because it would destroy. In its prison, the Minotaur demanded to be fed, and all that would satisfy was human flesh. This dynamic is like a psychological complex that has taken control. The untamed energy of the Goddess leaves in its wake a trail of madness if it is not understood and integrated. It cannot remain repressed for it devours from within. It cannot be killed for it merely takes another form. At least in the labyrinth, it had a home and we knew where to find it. Once Theseus killed it, without befriending it, the Minotaur became a diffused energy that unconsciously permeated civilized life.

Theseus was able to penetrate the heart of the great secret. He was brave and strong, but not only bravery and strength were necessary. He was connected by the thread to Ariadne, representative of the Great Goddess and descendent of the moon goddess line. She fell in love with Theseus. What a gift for Theseus to be loved by such a woman, and yet as we see later, he shunned her. He did not know how to relate to this kind of power in a woman. He only knew how to overpower and kill.

This version of the myth had Ariadne give Theseus a sword, symbolic of the ability to kill, cut through, and reach the essence of something. The sword could have helped Theseus relate to the depths of the repressed unconscious, as represented by his and Ariadne's half brother the Minotaur. (The Minotaur and Ariadne share a mother, Pasiphae; the Minotaur and Theseus share a father, Poseidon.) Many say Ariadne was rejected by Theseus and some versions of the myth speak of her suicide as a result of sorrow. This appears to be a patriarchal rationalization that does not want to give her the credit for choosing Dionysus, the great God of passion and transformation, over Theseus, for whom relationship seemed to be so expendable. I say good for her!

There are other versions of the myth that have Ariadne giving Theseus a light so he could see into the darkness. In that version, Theseus fought the Minotaur with his bare hands. That is closer to what needed to happen, but he still ended by killing the Minotaur.

There are many opportunities offered and missed in this myth. Perhaps it was time for something to change. It was time for King Minos not to want to be subservient to Poseidon (the great unconscious), but when the powers of Eros are so damaged they must be relearned. It all seems to have to do with power over, rather than power from within. The Minotaur is a great power contained within, and can be likened to a powerful unconscious complex that devours the life force of a person because it had been caged in the unconscious and not allowed the light of day. The Minotaur did not need to be killed, but befriended and integrated. It was not yet the time for Theseus to do this.

The call comes from the center of the labyrinth, which contains the shadow side of the drive for life and the dark side of the life instinct that wants to be fed. Theseus has the help of the Feminine acting as guardian at the threshold. He is guided in and out by the thread under the power of the Great Goddess. He has the sword of opportunity.

What he does not have is the right attitude. He does not seem open to meet his half brother and get to know him. He knows there is a force that devours and his only solution is to kill it. Although this releases the people from its grip, it also destroys the kingdom of Crete, resulting in King Minos' death, and leads to many tragedies for Theseus himself. Theseus is unable to relate to the world with his feminine nature healed and his shadow incorporated. There is death but no rebirth. Theseus' preparation for his entry was insufficient. Ariadne's assistance is premature and is first used and then abused.

Nicole's Story

What follows is the story of "Nicole," a woman in her mid-forties, who tells us in her own words how she met her Minotaur in the analytical process and was able to embrace and integrate him. In a series of psychodramas, unbeknownst to her conscious awareness at the time, she re-enacted Theseus' encounter with the Minotaur but with a different conclusion.

> I have had many years of analysis and feel like I touched the centre more than once, but this time was deeper and more powerful than any before. I had been feeling full of rage—but not at anything in particular. I wanted mainly to smash glass. I was terrified that I was going to go mad—that if I allowed myself to experience these feelings they would pull me over an edge from which there was no return.
>
> I explained to my analyst that I felt my rage taking the form of a beast that wanted to give in to and express these emotions. In order to hold the energy, we created a sacred space in which I could safely let the beast "live" and, if it got too much for me, I could move out of the space and sit in a chair we designated as the safe chair. My analyst was to be my witness.
>
> I became the beast and let the beast overcome me for that period of time. I took off my shoes, let my hair loose, covered my body with a large blanket, and the monster spoke. It danced. It pounced. It screeched out the poisons in its blood. It writhed. It sobbed. It screamed of the terror of staying in its caged centre and the terror of coming out. Both felt like they would bring death. Both were intolerable. It warned the world that it was more powerful than anyone and that anyone coming near would do so at their peril. At the same time, the longing to get

out and be allowed to live was palpable.

Between sessions, the rage was powerfully present but controlled. Images of destruction paraded in and out of my consciousness. I wanted to pound things. I wanted to smash things. I wanted to shatter glass. I wanted to push people's faces in and kick men's balls off and destroy the world! I allowed the images as much life as I could bear and knew there had to be a way for me to express this rage in a contained manner. I created for myself a sword made of rolled-up newspaper.

In my next session, the beast appeared again. This time, it was so full of rage that an inner madness threatened. Could I allow the beast full reign, knowing that it was also partly human? I thrashed and pounded with the sword, and screamed, cursing all those who had hurt me, spewing out hatreds I had dared not acknowledge, releasing a flood of venom I could not previously have borne. When I was spent, I lay sobbing on the bed, still in the centre, warning my analyst that if anyone came in now that the guardian beast had been heard, felt, and acknowledged, and somehow depotentiated—if anyone came in now and hurt me—I would die. Every pore of my being felt the truth of that statement. It was, thankfully, a terror I was able to hold.

I felt like my heart was made of glass—fragile and breakable. I felt like I had carried around that heart of glass all my life and could not bear either too much warmth or too much cold. After a lifetime of suffering, I knew something was coming to an end. By exposing to the world the roaring bars of my cage, I had also broken them down.

There were still flashes of rage between that session and the next but not so prevalent or dominant. In my next analytical session, when the Minotaur beast emerged, it was enraged with God. Why hadn't God saved me? I told a story of my entire life spent with the most important parts of me behind the bars of that cage. Another part of me had lived and searched, traveled around the world, looked for what was missing, and wanted someone to reunite me with the life spark so I could feel at home at last. The pain in the moment exploded as I remembered so many times in the past of hope that ultimately ended in betrayal and disappointment. It was as if, back then, I had had no inner container to hold what I had experienced. The despair became greater and greater as the number of journeys increased and the failures multiplied. Much of this grief poured forth in this session, together with the unspeakable terror of being disappointed again.

To my amazement, something then shifted. I could feel it in my body. My heart was no longer glass but a pumping, fleshy, flexible muscle. In the safe chair I looked into the eyes of my analyst and no longer saw danger and death mirrored there. I saw a friend, an ally. We had done it. The Minotaur seemed gone. Maybe it had been given a heart like the Tin Man in the Wizard of Oz and been humanized. If death is a transformation from one state of being to another, then we had succeeded for the moment in killing or transforming one haunted and haunting Minotaur.

It took Nicole a long time to meet and expose her Minotaur in all its raw power. Like the time it takes to traverse the labyrinth, that was essential. A story had to be told; without the story there is no context. A container had to be built; without the container there is no safety. Defenses had to be acknowledged and respected, for without their acknowledgment and respect there can be no trust. Trust had to be allowed to grow, not a trust in the mind of the adult but a trust that had to seep back down into the cells of the infant who thirsted after it but dared not let it in. Time, patience, courage, the possibility of embodiment, and a deep and intuitive understanding of the archetypal structures we were dealing with, led to the transformation of her Minotaur. Her rage is no longer Minotaur-like and at the mercy of an archaic, infantile layer of her psyche. It is now in the service of the mature woman she is becoming.

Nicole's powerful story is an example of the transformative potential of meeting our inner Minotaur and engaging with him, not killing him. All the elements of Theseus' confrontation with the Minotaur are present. The Minotaur is in a caged and protected space, difficult to reach. There is great danger involved in doing so. A space with an entrance and an exit was created; the path in and out in this case is known. Ariadne and her thread are represented by the analyst's presence and his voice was a means of connection to reality that the adult part of Nicole could hang onto. The sword came from Nicole's unconscious and gave her the opportunity to cut through the bars of the cage to see what was inside and outside. Nicole was both the Minotaur and the one in danger from the Minotaur. She does not kill him the way Theseus did, but by embodying him she allowed him to transform.

> So few grains of happiness
> measured against all the dark
> and still the scales balance.
> The world asks of us
> only the strength we have and we give it.
> then it asks more, and we give it.[2]
> —*Jane Hirshfield*

2. Jane Hirshfield, excerpted from "The Weighing," in *The October Palace*, p. 79.

Triple Goddess constellation: Persephone, Demeter, and Hecate.

7

DEMETER AND PERSEPHONE

The goddess becomes a mother, rages and grieves over the Kore who was ravished in her own being, the Kore whom she immediately recovers, and in whom she gives birth to herself again. The idea of the original Mother-Daughter goddess, at root a single entity, is at the same time the idea of rebirth.[1]

—Karl Kerenyi

We could therefore say that every mother contains her daughter in herself and every daughter her mother, and that every woman extends backwards into her mother and forwards into her daughter.[2]

—C. G. Jung

The Demeter and Persephone myth is one of the most well known and frequently described descent myths, and it gives us

1. Karl Kerenyi, *Eleusis*, p.123.
2. C. G. Jung, *Collected Works*, 9i, par. 316.

more insight into the labyrinth journey. It is about healing of the Feminine, for within it our triple-goddess nature is united.

To understand the progression of human consciousness as seen in myths, we need to look at their historical context. The Inanna poem (see Chapter 8) most likely originated in Sumer about 4000 B. C., before patriarchal orientation wielded its stranglehold on the goddess cultures. In that poem, we are presented with a strong woman who chooses to make the great journey to connect with the dark. Aegean civilization, however, made tentative beginnings in the third millennium, reached its height toward 1600 B. C., then spread from Crete to continental Greece. The myth of Demeter and Persephone was written no later than 650 B. C. With it we have patriarchal influence and the concomitant difference in the approach toward women and the Feminine. Persephone is raped into the underworld, rather than choosing to journey forth.

The Persephone Story

The story unfolds as follows.[3] Persephone is playing in the meadow with other young goddesses and is attracted to a large, beautiful narcissus planted there by Gaia (her grandmother). As Persephone stretches out her hands to pick the flower, the earth opens up and Hades (her father Zeus' brother and therefore her uncle), King of the Underworld, grabs Persephone and carries her away in his golden chariot.

Characters in the Myth of Demeter and Persephone

Persephone ...... Daughter of Demeter and Zeus
Demeter .... Mother of Persephone, wife of Zeus
Hecate .... Crone of the Triple Goddess, goddess of the
crossroads
Zeus .... King of the Upper World, brother of Hades
Hades .... King of the Underworld

3. Charles Boer, *The Homeric Hymns: The Charles Boer Translation.*

King Celeus . . . . . . King of Eleusis
Metanira . . . . Wife of King Celeus, mother of Demophoon
Hermes . . . . God of transition
Perceptive Iambe . . Baubo, a household servant

Persephone screams to her father for help, but the only ones who hear are Hecate and the Sun. We find out that Zeus, who is far away receiving offerings from his people, had planned it all. Finally, the echo of Persephone's cries reaches her mother, Demeter, whose heart is seized with pain. No one would tell Demeter the truth, and for nine days she did not eat, drink, or bathe. Hecate appears on the ninth day and tells her that she heard Persephone being abducted but saw nothing. Together they approach the Sun, who describes how Hades abducted Persephone under Zeus' direction. He exhorts Demeter to not grieve but to be happy about Persephone's wonderful marriage.

Demeter's grief becomes even deeper. She leaves the company of the gods and wanders among human beings. Dressed like an old woman to disguise her beauty, she arrives in Eleusis. There, at the well, she meets the daughters of King Celeus. When questioned about who she was and where she was from, Demeter tells a tale. She says her name is Doso, that she had just crossed the sea from Crete, having been captured to be sold. When everyone was feasting she escaped, did not know where she now was, and would like to find work as a nurse. The sisters, recognizing that Demeter was special, offer her work looking after their young brother Demophoon, who was "long desired and much loved."

Veiled and grieving, Demeter follows the girls to their home, and as she crosses the threshold the doorway becomes filled with divine light. Metanira (the girls' mother) gets up to greet her. Demeter does not want to sit on a "splendid couch" but takes her mourning further, finally sitting on a chair brought to her by "Perceptive Iambe" (Baubo). She sits there wasting away until Baubo cheers her with bawdy jokes. Demeter refuses the sweet wine offered by Metanira, and asks instead for barley water and pennyroyal. She gladly accepts the position of looking after Demophoon.

Demeter treats Demophoon as if he were a god. She anoints

him with ambrosia, and at night, in secret, holds him over a powerful fire. The child thrives without food, begins to look like the gods and would in time have become immortal like them. Metanira, spying one night, screams in terror for her son as she sees him put into the flames. Demeter is furious. She throws the child to the ground and calls them stupid people, saying they don't even know "when fate is bringing them something good or something bad." She curses the sons of Eleusis saying they will make war on each other forever.

Now Doso identifies herself as Demeter and demands that a temple be built in her honor. She says she will inaugurate the mysteries herself. The family try to appease the goddess even though they are shaking with fear. The temple is built and Demeter installs herself there for a year, wasting away with longing for her daughter. She stops all seeds from growing and creates a terrible famine. This finally catches Zeus' attention, as he is being deprived of offerings from the people.

Zeus sends all the gods and goddesses, in turn, to try to persuade Demeter to come back to the gods from the world of men. She refuses until she can see the beautiful face of her daughter again. Zeus hears this and sends Hermes to "exhort Hades with soft words" to release Persephone. Hermes finds the couple reclining on their couches. Hades is more than willing to let Persephone go, telling her when she is with him she will be a respected ruler of his land. He gives her a sweet pomegranate seed, which she eats. This is to ensure that she will come back to him.

The reunion between Demeter and Persephone is joyous and emotional. The first question Persephone is asked is if she ate anything in the underworld. When Demeter gets an affirmative answer, she decrees that Persephone will spend one-third of the year in the underworld and two-thirds in the upper world. Persephone tells all. Then Hecate joins them and from that day on, "that lady precedes and follows Persephone." Thus we have the Triple Goddess constellated, Zeus consents to the arrangement for Persephone, and the crops began to grow again. Demeter reveals her mysteries and commands they be honored forevermore.

The Wisdom of the Myth

In this myth, we have the Triple Goddess depicting the three levels of the Feminine within each of us: Persephone as the Maiden, Demeter as the Mother, and Hecate as the Crone.

Persephone represents innocence, reaching out to the narcissus which symbolizes beauty, truth, and self-knowledge. She is cavorting in the garden with her friends when the rape occurs. We are all innocents in this world, helpless against the vagaries of fate. One example from many that occurred while I was writing this was the collapse of the dance floor at a wedding party in Jerusalem that killed and injured people and changed lives forever. Whenever we *suddenly* find ourselves in the dark of the underworld, we have symbolically been raped. We lose our ingenuousness and come face-to-face with the Dark Goddess. She teaches us about the unpredictability of life and the inevitability of human suffering and death.

Rape is a brutal act perpetrated by one person on an unwilling other. Rape on the physical plane is always a devastating wrong, while rape on the psychic plane rips away the veils of illusion and shocks us into another way of being. Rape can be Soul destroying if it throws us too violently into the terrors of a chaotic personal or archetypal underworld. This underworld is alien because it has been cut off from consciousness for so long. It is feared because it is so powerful.

Persephone fights. She does not know what is happening to her. She expresses terror, anguish, and rage at being abducted, abandoned, betrayed, and abused, but her feelings and their expression go with her unheard to the dark world of Hades. Persephone doesn't know if anyone hears her cries for help. Perhaps this is the most terrifying aspect of being raped into the underworld—feeling totally and utterly alone.

Several years ago I observed a psychodrama that evolved into an enactment of this part of the myth. The protagonist, a woman, was on the floor in a trance-like state. Another woman was calling her name. As consciousness slowly returned, the protagonist looked to see where the voice was coming from, and at the same time reached out to hold onto a tiny bag the other woman wore around her neck. Unbeknownst to the protagonist, the bag contained a Druid bell. The woman who wore the bell gently said, "Yes, I will ring the bell so that you can find your way back." The protagonist burst into tears and realized that was where her terror lay! She was afraid of getting lost in the underworld and not being able to find her way out.

This is a repeated theme in each of the myths told here. To be able to descend into the dark places and return, we must have someone left behind to hold the thread, light the torch, ring the bell, or go for help when necessary. This knowledge allows us to sink into the experience and learn, for we are no longer terrified that we will be left there forever.

If Persephone is innocence, then Hecate is wisdom. She is mistress of the black arts, witchcraft, and spells that bind. She is the Goddess of the Dark Moon and of mediumistic intuition in women. The cave, her home, is so often associated with the womb that it seems Hecate holds the knowledge of the earth womb in her being. She knows the cry of Persephone because it is familiar to her. She has been where Persephone is. She knows the underworld places and grounds the experience for the other parts of us. She knows the process. She lets Demeter sit with her grief for nine days (nine being the number for new birth) before approaching her. She does not rush Demeter but helps hold her in her anguish.

Demeter, on the other hand, is the visible part of us that deals with the outside world and acts for us there. When Persephone goes underground and we are not connected with Hecate, Demeter is bereft. Therefore it is important to understand Demeter's story. Demeter seems to go through three stages. First she is in mourning and does not eat or drink. She appears to be in a state of shock. This is how we feel when we have been traumatized, as if a life force we have relied upon has gone. We no longer know who we are or what world we are living in. All the parameters that used to ground us are missing.

At this point, Demeter does not know what has happened to Persephone and is deeply feeling her loss. After nine days she is told by Hecate that Persephone has been abducted but she did not know by whom. Now, both women go immediately to the Sun, who sees all and represents clear consciousness. In response to Demeter's pleading, he tells her the truth while at the same time making light of her grief. This to me is a classical patriarchal response—denying the realm of emotion and of the dark—relying only on logic. Demeter now has a name for her grief and moves more deeply into her depression.

In this second stage, Demeter leaves the world of the gods and joins the world of humans. She creates a new personality for herself. This is not an unknown ploy in the human realm as we attempt to escape something overwhelming. We might feel that a change is all we need, and so we change jobs, partners, cities, or friends, but we soon learn that we have brought our pain with us. The depth of Demeter's depression becomes apparent when she returns to King Celeus' home to take up her duty as a nursemaid. She is clothed in black and sits in silence, not talking, not laughing, not moving. Demeter's refusal to sit on the splendid couch is further indication of her mournful state. In Judaism, mourners are not allowed to sit on soft chairs or sofas.

It is only through "Perceptive Iambe" (or Baubo, a household servant), that the scene begins to change. Bruce Lincoln brings out a fascinating point when he discusses how Clement of Alexandria described this incident.

> The raucous Baubo—whose name literally means 'vagina' or a 'mock vagina counterpart to a dildo' replaces the more sedate Iambe whose name is derived from the iambic meters used in all Greek jesting verse. Of Baubo Clement reports: Speaking thus she hoisted up her robes and displayed all of her body, a shape that was not fitting. And the child was there and he was laughing as he kept thrusting his hand under Baubo's breasts. And truly when the goddess (Demeter) saw this, she smiled in her Spirit and she took up the shining vessel in which the kykeon was contained.[4]

4. Bruce Lincoln, *Emerging from the Chrysalis*, p. 80.

This bawdy sexual humor brings Demeter back into her body, and it is what grounds us in the Feminine. There is power in raucous, feminine, sexual humor which we usually inhibit because it is not acceptable. When women gather together in the absence of men and this energy is present, the force of the sexuality is so great that it can no longer be suppressed, and it bursts forth in hilarity and wildness.

This brings Demeter sufficiently out of her depression to get on with caring for Demophoon. What is this interlude with Demophoon? Demeter is trying to "fix" something in the outside world by taking a human child and making him immortal. Is it to help her regain some of the power she lost in the face of Zeus (her husband) and Hades (her brother-in-law) colluding to abduct her daughter? We feel betrayed by the gods when we have been "raped." What do we do when we feel we have lost control? Some of us may try to defy the fates by participating in more dangerous or life-threatening behavior, as if to say, "get me if you can!" Many addictions are examples of this. When Demeter is confronted with her behavior, she becomes vindictive and full of rage. We suspect her actions toward Demophoon to be self-serving and in no way for his benefit.

Each time we go into the center of the labyrinth to symbolically die and be reborn, we are getting used to death. Immortality is not a state we strive for after we are dead, but as we live. It does not mean that we surpass death; it means we embrace it. Demeter is attempting to give the child something that would separate him from his human nature and destiny. It would deprive him of the motivational and creative power of human suffering and mortality. It mirrors how she is trying to save herself from the pain of her loss and the powerlessness she feels. It gives her a taste of what it is like to be human.

This leads us into the third stage of the mourning process. Demeter orders a temple built for herself and sits in her rage and anguish. She is now able to sink into the feelings from which she has been running. She is in the center of the labyrinth, the place where we face our inner demons. For one year Demeter sits there in a time of inertia. Although she does not go out into the world, she is still able to express her rage at Zeus through the people. She stops all crops from growing, that is, all outward expression of her productivity and creativity. For a woman who has always been active and productive, this is a very difficult period of her process. In the myth, this would have gone on until humankind was wiped out but Zeus finally took notice. Without mankind and the crops, there was no way homage could be paid to him. There comes a point in the process when our healing has been done and we realize we have had enough of fallowness. It is time to wind our way slowly back out of the labyrinth to meet life from a new state of being.

Notice how Demeter approaches Zeus by withholding and waiting, not by direct confrontation. Demeter's stubbornness and determination are admirable. Sometimes the internal and external forces we need to overcome in order to redeem lost parts of ourselves are formidable and require ingenious tactics and perseverance. Demeter has that and models it for us. It is important to remember how necessary the Masculine element is to boundary the Feminine.

Just as Enki sends messengers to the underworld (see Inanna in Chapter 8), so does Zeus. Hermes (the God who travels between worlds, the messenger) is sent to retrieve Persephone. Persephone, however, eats the pomegranate seed before her departure, which ensures her return. This parallels Inanna's being told that she must find someone to replace her in the underworld if she is to be released. Demeter, once she faces the inevitable, declares that Persephone would spend three months of every year (some versions say six) in the underworld and the rest of the time above ground with her. The cyclical quality of life is finally, albeit reluctantly, acknowledged and accepted. We need our winters of fallowness and our renewal in the dark to move creatively into the light. The myth is warning us that we must not lose touch with the elemental, underworld nature of our being. It is a model of healing, for in the end the Triple Goddess is reunited. Here is a description of what follows this unification within the Feminine which readies us for union with the Masculine.

When we relate to the Triple Goddess fact of ourselves we will initially be perturbed by her changeability. The centuries of patriarchal, rigid, one-dimensional, abstract thinking struggle against her, rejecting her impulses as "chaotic" and leading to an inner anarchy. But as we change inwardly and the patterns of our Souls mold to her formative energies we will see her more clearly. We will come to value a consciousness of cyclical change within ourselves. Once we have come to an inner relationship with the Feminine, we can begin the process of uniting the Masculine and Feminine facets of our Souls. This, the true Mystical Marriage, the Conjunction of Opposites, is the most exciting and valuable adventure that any human being can undertake. Out of the Conjunction, this inner meeting and integration, can arise such a powerful current of creative energy as few have ever experienced. If humanity could collectively embark on this journey, great creative energy would be released, and we could render ourselves true vessels for the Spiritual energies of the future.[5]

The following was dreamt by a woman in her mid-fifties who has been struggling with the integration of the Persephone part of herself (her daughter and the baby girl), the Hecate part (the old woman), and the Demeter part (the dream ego that is active).

I was going to visit some friends. I arrived with a beautiful baby girl and my older daughter. I looked at the baby's face. She had beautiful eyes and a round, pink mouth that looked wet. I felt so much love for her. She looked at me and smiled. I remembered her diapers were dirty and I hadn't changed her before, thinking I would do it once we got to the house, but I forget. I get lost in old feeling of resentment and anger.

I hear the baby crying very loudly. My older daughter was with her and reminded me that I hadn't changed her diapers. I run to the baby and feel very badly I had left her dirty for so long. I pick her up and hold her tight and put her down on a

5. Adam McLean, *The Triple Goddess*, p.12.

changing table. There I remove her diaper and wipe her bum. She stops crying. I feel much closer to her than before and rewarded to have such a beautiful baby. She was very patient, tender, and loving and I loved her with all my heart.

In the above section of the dream, the dreamer is connecting with a young, vulnerable part of herself, but she is reluctant to clean the baby's diaper, the "shit" of her life, in an honest and integral way instead of indulging in self-pity. Although the baby has been in the safe-keeping of her daughter (a part of her inner Feminine that has developed), she needs to deal with the "shit." Once she does, she feels so much closer to the baby. The bond has been re-established. The dream continues.

I was with an old, old woman. Her face was very wrinkled and she appeared to be as old as the world. I was young, maybe 20 or 30 years old and I looked young and felt very insecure. Something worried me a lot . . . perhaps that we didn't have enough to eat. The old woman told me to come with her. It was night, and dark with only a beige-brown-yellow light. The place we were at looked very poor with huts made of clay or mud and unpaved streets. It looked like a poor rural town or an underdeveloped country from long ago.

I was at her side when we started to walk. When she moved, she looked stronger. She walked quickly and her body looked medium built with strong bones. I had to walk fast to keep up with her. We walked for a while until we went into a food store that also looked old and poor. There was a strong dark man who looked like an Arab standing in the store. There was a lot of dust all over the counters and on the floor but there was little food. The place was almost empty. The old woman saw a vegetable in a box that looked like a lettuce or cabbage; it was light green. She checked it out and said, "This is not what I want; we need good vegetables (food)."

I agreed with her. I needed a good source of energy—good food to feel better. Although I didn't say this to her, she knew what I needed. I felt she understood my problem. When she started to walk again she pulled me out of the store not by touching me, but by her force alone. She said, "I know of another store, of other places where we can find good fresh vegetables." And off we went.

She jumped into a car and started to drive very fast, going through winding roads in the dark or semi-dark, turning here and there. I was in a panic. I felt very insecure not knowing where we were going and having for a driver this old, old woman who was not wearing glasses. I didn't say much. I nodded a lot when she was talking. She was mostly talking to herself. Although I didn't understand all her mumbling, her voice was strong and showed command. The old woman knew what she was doing and she had a lot of experience driving in the dark. She could even see in the dark; meanwhile, I couldn't. I also understood that she knew the area very well. She was not lost at all. However, I wanted to know where we were going. It bothered me a lot that she was in control and not myself. I asked her a few times in a very soft voice. I didn't want to upset her; I knew that I depended on her to find the way out. Deep inside I decided to trust her.

After acknowledging and dealing with the "shit," the dreamer has this remarkable encounter with the Dark Goddess, who is older than the world, knows and sees in the dark, knows what is nourishing for the dreamer and what is not, and is willing to guide her. When deep inside she decides to trust her, we have a unification of the Feminine and the beginning of a profound change in this woman's life.

The Demeter and Persephone myth ends with the Triple Goddess re-established, the crops beginning to grow, and a declaration of the Eleusinian Mysteries (rites that were to be performed yearly). They lasted for more than 3,000 years, and in all that time the secret of what really transpired was never revealed. That in itself is phenomenal. Those who have researched the rites describe a process of initiation and ritual that lasted several days. The ultimate reward was the initiates' loss of their fear of death.

What has this myth added to our understanding of descent and return? It has reinforced the need for a link between the worlds: a loyal and caring person (Demeter) who holds the connection for the one who has descended (Persephone). In the myth of Inanna we will have another model of using patience and persistence for effecting change rather than direct confrontation (as in the myth of Theseus). We have learned the necessity of time for healing a "rape," that is, an unplanned, unexpected, traumatic, perhaps violent regression or descent. We have seen that healing comes from both the reunification of the Feminine and the intercession of the Masculine (albeit Zeus is a more reluctant and removed Masculine presence than Enki in the Inanna myth), and that this healing is not a finality but must be reinforced by a cyclical movement between the worlds.

> I have lived on the lip
> of insanity, wanting to know reasons,
> knocking on a door. It opens.
> I've been knocking from the inside![6]
> —*Rumi*

6. John Moyne and Coleman Barks, *Unseen Rain: Quatrains of Rumi*, p. 75.

Inanna, Queen of Sumeria.

8

INANNA

Inanna demands that we bow down, become submissive to her as giver of our fate. If we are fully open to her, we cannot avoid the suffering and tragedy that is woven into life. Inanna is not evil. She is the stark horror and beauty of what is. To open to her is to stretch oneself between the opposites.[1]

—Betty DeShong Meador

Who is Inanna and why is she so important to our understanding of the Feminine journey? She is the bridge between the Neolithic Great Mother and the biblical Eve, Sophia, and Mary, and the Shekinah of the Jewish Kabbalah. She is the Queen of Sumeria, The Queen of Heaven and Earth, and was also known by the name of Ishtar in Babylonia. Her story is at least 4,000 years old and until a hundred and fifty years ago, we knew little of Sumeria. The discovery of tablets in the ancient city of Nippur (in present-day Iraq) and their translations, has given us epic tales, hymns, and proverbs from those times.[2] The one that concerns us here is

1. Betty De Shong Meador, *Uncursing the Dark*, p.125.
2. See Diane Wolkenstein and Samuel Noah Kramer's *Inanna*, as well as Meador's *Uncursing the Dark*, for poem translations.

Inanna's descent to the underworld, but before we look at it let's explore who Inanna was and who she can be for us today.

Meador's book, *Inanna, Lady of the Largest Heart*, is deeply moving. Reading about Inanna and the devotion of her priestess, Enheduanna, gave me a feeling of coming home to myself, as if a template created four millennia ago was slowly being rediscovered today. The journey of Inanna, the archetypal Feminine goddess, embraces her multifaceted nature. Meador tells us that Inanna is "the element of chaos" that hangs over every situation. Inanna is not bounded by social order; she represents "the unthinkable thought," and confronts us with ourselves.[3]

> Inanna's presence draws us into the realm of the inner life. She is the guide who insists we face our shadowy contradictions, that we own who we really are in our painful and wonderful complexity. As the Goddess of paradox she is the model of unity in multiplicity.[4]

Inanna's presence is important, but we can also learn from those who worshipped her. Meador brings us into the life of Enheduanna, who was appointed by her father, King Sargon, to the position of High Priestess. She served in this role for over 40 years.[5]

In her poems to Inanna we get a sense of deep love and compassion for the Goddess, and the way her inner journey echoed some aspects of Inanna's. Just as women today are descending to explore the richness of their inner lives, so did Enheduanna, through her relationship with Inanna, begin to discover her own individuality and uniqueness. Enheduanna serves as a model of what it means to live your life connected to the depth and breadth of the archetypal Feminine today. Her poetry will give us insight into her world and relationship with her goddess. The poems are complex and show great psychological depth and an amazing understanding of the diversity of the human condition.

3. Betty De Shong Meador, *Inanna: Lady of the Largest Heart*, p. 21.
4. Meador, *Inanna*, p. 22.
5. Meador, *Inanna*, p. 6.

This fragment from the poem *Inanna of the Largest Heart* gives us a sense of Inanna's formidable power.

> she speaks
> cities tumble
>> fall into ruined mounds
>> their houses haunted
>> their shrines barren
> the one who disobeys
> she does chase, twist
> afflict with jumbled eyes
>
> fighting hand to hand
> or hurling hurricane winds
> she alone is awesome
>
> fighting is her play
> she never tires of it
> she goes out running
> strapping on her sandals

ᘓ

> lioness Inanna
> crouched in a reed thicket
> leaps to slash the fearless
>
> mountain wildcat
> prowling the roads
> shows wet fangs
> gnashes her teeth
>
> wild bull Queen
> mistress of brawn
> boldly strong
> no one dares turn away[6]

ᘓ

6. Meador, pp. 120–121.

where she spits venom
fighting erupts
tumult spreads the poison

her overturned fury
Holy Woman's rage
is a rampaging flood
hands cannot dam

a ditch of spilling water
she floods over a road
swamps the one she loathes[7]

ᴣ

woe the city under her frown
its fields lie barren[8]

ᴣ

SHE
in the midst of havoc
shouting over the din
begins her sacred song
the song drawn with a stick
carves her indelible scheme
she sings

> her bread is lamentation
> her milk is weeping
> bread and milk of death
> O Inanna
> bread and milk of death
> who eats it will not last

> who she feeds burns with pain of gall
> gags on dung

7. Meador, p. 119.
8. Meador, p. 119.

her song sung
with joy of heart
in the plain
with joy of heart
she sings
and soaks her mace
in blood and gore
smashes heads
butchers prey
with eater-ax and
bloodied spear
all day
these evil blades
the warrior flings
pours blood on offerings
so who she feeds
dines on death[9]

꒜

to heap on lavish adornments
small   large   fine   wide
are your Inanna[10]

꒜

to utter slander
words of deception
to speak unashamedly
even hostilely
are yours Inanna

to sneer at an answer
false or true
to say wicked words
are yours Inanna

9. Meador, pp.120–121.
10. Meador, p.129.

to joke   inflame a quarrel
provoke laughter
to defile   to esteem
are yours Inanna

calamity   bitter woes
torment   wickedness
darkening the light
are yours Inanna[11]

ノ

to be all knowing
is yours Inanna

to build a bird's nest
safe in a sound branch
make indestructible
are yours Inanna

to lure snakes from the wasteland
terrorize the hateful
throw in chains   hold in bondage
are yours Inanna

to summon the hated
is yours Inanna

to cast lots
is yours Inanna

to gather the scattered
restore the living place
are yours Inanna
setting free
is yours Inanna[12]

11. Meador, p. 129.
12. Meador, pp. 129–130.

One gets a sense of the many paradoxes in Inanna's nature, for such is the nature of the Feminine. It protects life while at the same time causing death. The imagery is beautiful and strangely relevant to us more than 4,000 years later.

The Inanna Story

Inanna's descent to the underworld was perhaps the most famous epic poem of that time. It portrays Inanna's meeting with her sister, Erishkigal. Like the Greek mysteries of Eleusis that enacted Persephone's descent to the underworld and subsequent rescue by Demeter, so this mythic drama may have been re-enacted in the Sumerian temples that served as both womb and tomb for the Goddess.[13]

Characters in the Myth of Inanna

Inanna . . . . Queen of Heaven
Erishkigal . . . . Inanna's sister, Queen of the Underworld
Gugalanna . . . . Erishkigal's husband, Great Bull of Heaven
Dumuzi . . . . Inanna's husband
Ninshubur . . . . Inanna's handmaid
Neti . . . . Gatekeeper
Nanna . . . . Inanna's father
Enlil . . . . Inanna's paternal grandfather
Enki . . . . Inanna's maternal grandfather,
              God of Wisdom
Galaturra . . . . Androgynous creature
Kurgarra . . . . Androgynous creature
Shara, Lulal . . . . . . Inanna's sons
Geshtinanna . . . . . Inanna's sister

Here is the story. Inanna is the Queen of Heaven and Earth. Her older sister, Erishkigal, is Queen of the Underworld. Inanna turns her "ear to great earth" and decides to go down to visit her sister and be there for the mourning of her sister's husband

13. Anne Baring and Jules Cashford, *The Myth of the Goddess*, p. 185.

Gugalanna, "The Great Bull of Heaven." Inanna makes great preparations for her descent. First, she lets go of all her connections in the upper world, naming them one by one. There are seven. Then she takes her servant girl, Ninshubur, with her and gives very explicit instructions. If Inanna does not return in three days then Ninshubur is to "cry in lamentation," play the drum, wander through the houses of the gods, tear at her body, and wear rags. She is to go into mourning. Then she is to visit in turn, until one responds, Enlil (the father of Inanna's father and the Director of the Rational World), Nanna (Inanna's father), and finally Enki (Inanna's mother's father and the God of Wisdom). She is to beg for their assistance in saving Inanna's life.

Inanna goes to the gates of the underworld and knocks. The gatekeeper, Neti, asks her to identify herself and her purpose. She replies that she has come alone to be with Erishkigal at her husband's funeral. Neti consults with Erishkigal and describes the sacred powers Inanna has brought with her, symbolized in the jewels and royal robes she is wearing. Erishkigal demands that the seven gates be closed and that Inanna be required to shed something at each gate until she is naked at the final one. Only then will she be allowed into the underworld.

> At each gate another item is taken from Inanna, She asks
> "What is this?"
> and each time is answered by Neti
>> "Quiet, Inanna, the ways of the underworld are perfect
>> They may not be questioned."[14]

Naked and bowed, Inanna enters the throne room and is tried by the judges of the underworld.

> Then Erishkigal fastened on Inanna the eye of death,
> She spoke against her the word of wrath.
> She uttered against her the cry of guilt.
> She struck her.

14. Wolkstein and Kramer, p. 58.

Inanna was turned into a corpse
A piece of rotting meat,
And was hung from a hook on the wall.[15]

After three days, Ninshubur follows the instructions exactly as
given by Inanna. She is refused by both Enlil, Inanna's grandfather, and Nanna, her father. Assuming she has gone desiring the
underworld powers, they say that it is forbidden to do so. They
infer that it was her fault for daring to go there in the first place.

Enki, her maternal grandfather and the God of Wisdom, under-
stands the danger Inanna is in and is deeply troubled by it. He
takes dirt from under his fingernails and makes two androgynous
creatures—a Kurgarra and a Galaturra. He gives them the "life-
giving water" and the "life-giving plant," and instructs them to
creep into the underworld. They will see Erishkigal and she will be
moaning. They are to moan with her. She will be so pleased she
will offer them gifts which they are to refuse. They are to ask for
Inanna's body instead.

And so it happens:

Like flies, they slipped through the cracks of the gates.
They entered the throne room of the Queen of the Underworld.
No linen was spread over her body
Her breasts were uncovered.
Her hair swirled around her head like leeks.

Erishkigal was moaning: "Oh! Oh! My inside!"
        They moaned: "Oh! Oh! Your inside!"

She moaned: "Oh! Oh! My outside!"
        They moaned: "Oh! Oh! Your outside!"

She groaned: "Oh! Oh! My belly!"
        They groaned: "Oh! Oh! Your belly!"

She groaned: "Oh! Ohhhh! My back!!"
        They groaned: "Oh! Ohhhh! Your back!!"

15. Wolkstein and Kramer, p. 60.

She sighed: "Ah! Ah! My heart!"
They sighed: "Ah! Ah! Your heart!"

She sighed: "Ah! Ahhhh! My liver!"
They sighed: "Ah! Ahhhh! Your liver!"[16]

Erishkigal stops and looks at them and asks them who they are. If they are gods, she says she will bless them; if they are mortals, she will give them a gift. They ask for the "corpse that hangs from the hook on the wall." Their request is granted. They sprinkle the food and water of life over Inanna and she comes back to life.

Inanna immediately wants to depart, but is told that "no one can leave the underworld unscathed." If she wishes to leave, Inanna must replace herself in the underworld. Surrounded by demons, Inanna leaves and meets Ninshubur at the gate to the underworld. The demons want to take Ninshubur but Inanna refuses, pointing out how Ninshubur both obeyed and mourned her. The same happens when they visit Inanna's two sons, Shara and Lulal.

When they come to Dumuzi, Inanna's husband and the king, they find him on his throne, content with his royal powers and not a sign of grief or welcome from him. Inanna cries out, "Sacrilege! Carry him away!"

The story continues with Dumuzi going through his suffering and letting go of his upper-worldly accoutrements. Utu, Inanna's brother, turns Dumuzi into a snake but still the demons pursue him. Finally he finds his sister, Geshtinanna, who weeps with him and interprets a dream that predicts his end. She is tortured by the demons who come looking for Dumuzi, but she does not reveal his location. Finally, with great compassion and sacrifice, she offers to share his time in the underworld. Inanna, moved by compassion for Geshtinanna and sorrow for Dumuzi, agrees that Geshtinanna and Dumuzi will each spend six months of the year in the underworld.

16. Wolkstein and Kramer, pp. 64-67.

The Wisdom of the Myth

Inanna is the Evening Star, the Judge, the Queen of the Land and its Fertility, the Goddess of War, the Goddess of Sexual Love, the Healer, the Life-giver, and the Composer of Songs.

Inanna's ear is to the ground. She "hears" something from the underworld. She hears the "call." She intuits that this is a place she needs to go. If Erishkigal is Inanna's dark side, then it is time for her to meet that part of herself. We need to look at Inanna's awareness of the dangers of this journey, the precautions she takes, and the preparations she makes.

First of all, Inanna enumerates everything she is in the upper world. This is a way of claiming her extroverted ego strengths and accomplishments. We need to have a strong sense of who we are in order to enter the underworld for the purpose of transformation and to be able to return. We cannot be stripped if there is nothing there to be stripped away.

Inanna plans very carefully, instructing Ninshubur in great detail about what to do if she fails to return. Getting left in the underworld happens. People who have not returned from madness have not had a person, or a thread (Theseus), by which they could find their way back or be rescued before it was too late. For this part of the journey we need to be accompanied by someone skilled enough to contain our experience. This can be an analyst or therapist, or sometimes a community of people organized to provide the container and lifeline while a person is in descent. If a part of ourselves remains conscious of the process while at the same time being immersed in it, this is preferable. What we learn from this myth is the importance of adequate preparation.

What does it mean that Ninshubur is Inanna's handmaid and not her mother (Demeter and Persephone) or sister? A handmaid or servant does not have blood ties, and therefore does not have the intricate and intimate emotional connections present in members of the same family. This gives her a certain objectivity and emotional distance—similar to an analyst. Ninshubur is also paid and presumably her loyalty is more guaranteed than the emotion-laden vagaries of the family.

Inanna has a reason for her descent. Outwardly it is to go the funeral of a Masculine element; inwardly it is to discover Erishkigal, her repressed dark Feminine. Having a purpose is essential. For women today, this often comes in the form of intense pain that leads downward and inward. We might not know exactly why we are going, but we know there is no choice. We must meet what is blocking us from life, and continuing life the way we have thus far is unbearable. Therefore we will risk all, for what we have sought and found thus far is no longer sufficient.

In the Hero's journey, we began with the "call." If the call is answered, there are guardians at the threshold to ensure the person is ready to proceed. Inanna meets Neti the Gatekeeper, and by answering his questions correctly she gets permission from Erishkigal to enter. But Erishkigal's terms are ruthless.

The process moves slowly. There are seven gates (as there are seven turns in each quadrant of the Chartres labyrinth and seven chakras in the human body). At each gate, Inanna is stripped of another part of her upper-world identity. Inanna protests, and is told it is part of the process. We cannot hurry or direct the descent. If we do hurry it, we are in danger of never returning or of aborting what is about to happen. Holding the labyrinth in mind as a sacred temenos allows us to be present for what will unfold, and know we will be safe.

Like the slow walking of the labyrinth, the slow stripping is important. As we die to ourselves as we have known ourselves, we slowly absorb and express the accompanying pain. Our bodies need to get used to the assimilation and expression of powerful emotions that can initially threaten to overwhelm our nervous systems. There can be a conscious fear of going mad. That is why the process is so slow. We are preparing ourselves for the anguish of final death and that time on the meat hook.

Time on the meat hook is difficult for anyone. It is the ultimate inertia, showing itself in depression, lethargy, despair, and complete impotence. We need to wait. Just as Demeter waited for one year before she was able to get Persephone's release, so Inanna needs to spend time on the meat hook, in the place of death and suffering, until it is time for rebirth. Erishkigal will not easily give up those she has claimed. This is quite different from the Hero fighting his way out.

Who is Erishkigal? She is Queen of the Underworld (like Persephone is of the Greek underworld, but very different!). Erishkigal did not choose the underworld but was given it for her domain. The Minotaur also did not choose to be in the center of the labyrinth.

According to Wolkstein, Erishkigal

> . . . eats clay and drinks dirty water. She has no compassion for the relationships of others, husband and wife or parent and child. Her one great craving is for her sexual satisfaction. . . . Like Lillith her sexuality is compulsive, insatiable, and without relationship or offspring.
>
> This underground goddess, whose realm is dry and dark, whose husband is dead, who has no protective or caring mother, father, or brother (that we know of), who wears no clothes, and whose childhood is lost, can be considered the prototype of the witch—unloving, unloved, abandoned, instinctual, and full of rage, greed, and desperate loneliness.[17]

But Erishkigal has tremendous power, the ultimate power, the power of Death. She and the Minotaur eat human flesh and neither she nor he have concern for relationship. They each are angry, lonely, and desperate to get their needs met and express their rage at any cost.

Erishkigal, as the shadow of Inanna, is a tragic figure. She is the shadow of many women who have been abused and wounded and are being eaten alive by their repressed horrors while being nice and accommodating in the outside world. Not only that, she is also the shadow of Patriarchal Woman, the one who has bought the story told to her by patriarchy. As a result, she denies the parts of her that don't fit the patriarchal value system. Many of us are not even conscious of having made this agreement. The Erishkigal part of us needs to be faced. She needs to scream out her agony and her rage. She needs to be moaned with. She needs to be integrated, not

17. Wolkstein and Kramer, p. 158.

killed as the Minotaur was. If we make ourselves conscious of her, we regain her power in our lives rather than being at the mercy of her anguish and desperation.

What follows is an extremely graphic passage written by a woman as she dared to imagine and record what the Erishkigal in her might be like. Most of us would not allow ourselves to enter the place she describes, and yet the experience of doing so was both freeing and healing for her.

> Here I am. I am in the centre. The air crackles with putrid, sickening smells. All is dark and foul. There is no natural light in this place, only murky blackness and the stench of burning and rotting flesh.
>
> I sit in the centre and I am like the little stone statue of the Irish Sheila. I sit crouched down with my legs apart and I hold the labia of my vagina, hold them apart for the world to see. On my face is an expression of malevolent evil. I snarl, I cackle, I shriek, I look down and I look up, and I shout in a voice so evil even the dead shudder in their graves. I shriek into the void. "I HAVE A DEAD AND EMPTY WOMB" . . . and I say that over and over and over again. And then I look down again and I see no, it is not empty, it is full of maggots and maggots are crawling out of my vagina, millions of maggots, millions of slimy maggots and I just look down between my legs and I am not surprised. I look and bend closer and closer until my mouth is at the entrance of my vagina and I begin to eat these millions of little maggots. I inhale them like a vacuum cleaner. They are my food, my nourishment. I am disgusted but I cannot stop. These maggots are my blood. They live in my veins. I can't let them get away.
>
> And as my head gets closer and closer to the opening, waves of noxious, nauseating fumes overwhelm me and I begin to vomit into the maggots at the same time as I am inhaling them, until I get so close to the vagina that my head begins to be sucked up inside. I am being pulled up inside myself. The ultimate uroborous. The ultimate in narcissistic copulation! I am a whole, a self, rolling around in the black pit of hell, and with each exhalation brown liquid seeps from my pores, runs down

my skin, liquid shit, the shit of the maggots, the shit of myself. And while all this is going on I laugh hysterically. I laugh at all the people I have fooled all my life. I laugh and I laugh and I laugh. I am human evil. I am an evil human soul.

I want to scratch people's eyes out. I want to take the talons that are my fingernails and rip them through the flesh of unsuspecting humans so that my evil will seep into their blood and the scars will mark them as one of mine. I want to sit on top of a staircase, sit with my naked bum hanging over the banister and shit and pee and shit and pee until there is nothing left inside of me and the sweet, holy smell of human self-righteousness is gone forever. I want to run naked down the street with my wild hair streaming behind me, and terrify people with the ugly truth of my evil-souled body. I want to bite off men's penises and jump on pregnant women's bellies.

I want to smear shit everywhere. I want to take it from my skin, from my rectum, and smear it on naked lovers making love, on plants and trees, and dogs and cats, and smiling faces, and holier-than-thou beatific countenances. I want to spit in people's faces so that they can taste and smell the putridness of who I am. I want to crawl over broken glass on my naked belly, and then I want to dance, to jump, to terrify all with this picture of excoriated, bloody, sagging female flesh. I want to shock the world!

I am so tired. So tired of pretending. So tired of being nice. So, so, so tired of hoping that someone would come along and save me from myself. Save me so that I would not have to go to this place of truth.

Speaking the unspeakable and owning our images and impulses in all their horror frees us from having to pretend that we could not possibly have feelings like this. At the same time it allows us to let go of the secret we have harbored—that at our core this is what we are. Many women share this awful dilemma. Because we are connected to this underworld place, because it is unspeakable and we know we have it inside of us waiting to be spoken, we see ourselves as identified with the abhorrent. By speaking it, we are freed to see that it is archetypal Feminine energy living in us, in other women, and perhaps men as well. We are "able to return safely to the very source of human sorrow, to the dark and threatening dimensions of being."[18]

What is this energy? It feels evil because it is so dark, but the images have to do with the flesh and its natural functions, with the creatures that inhabit the earth, and with feelings of rage at being stuck. We feel evil because we dare to connect to the forbidden. Others, with their "beatific countenances," seem to live in a world that denies, dismisses, demeans, and attempts to destroy a connection to what is natural. Those of us with a connection to that world can feel horrible about ourselves, and furious with those who keep us marginalized by threatening to burn us at the stake for such witchy energy.

Once we meet our inner Erishkigal, we no longer need to fear her. Look what happens as the story unfolds. Enki, the God of Wisdom, who takes the dirt from under his fingernails (something readily available, of the same substance as Erishkigal's world, and without gender), has been compared with the Greek God Poseidon in that they are both gods of the waters. Perera describes Enki as the generative, creative, playful, empathetic male."[19]

Enki has a deep understanding of Erishkigal, and we need to learn from him. He knows that Erishkigal wants, above all else, to be acknowledged and known. She can only experience that in a physical and emotional manner. She must be moaned with. Her pain must be echoed back to her in a guttural, nonverbal, primal way. Only then does she really feel seen. Only then can she trust that the moaning is true.

The profound desire of the Feminine is to be known, not analyzed. She wants to be known from the inside out, with quivering bellies, vibrating bodies, and tear-filled eyes. She wants every cell in our bodies to reverberate. Then she will communicate with us and grant our wishes. Then we can be grounded in her power.

This is the most significant part of the myth. It models an

18. Francoise O'Kane, *Sacred Chaos*, p. 54.
19. Sylvia Brinton Perera, *Descent to the Goddess*, p. 67.

approach other than the heroic, one appropriate to underworld descent that seeks to reclaim the Feminine rather than ravish or destroy her. She must be met in all her power and allowed to affect us to the point of dying to what we have been. We have to spend time with her in her domain, witness her agony and birthing process, and know all that is within us. When she knows that we know, she allows our release, leaving us forever changed. We come back with some of her ruthlessness and a power from within that no longer needs to, nor seeks to, dominate others. It knows that the ultimate and insuperable power is Death.

In Inanna's emergence she is told that "no one leaves the underworld unscathed." How true! Inanna is accompanied by demons who are there to ensure that someone takes her place, but Inanna also comes back ruthless. She spares those who have shown feeling for her (like Erishkigal spared Inanna because she was shown feeling), and condemns Dumuzi, her lover and husband, because he is invested in the power of his role over others and does not even get off his throne to greet Inanna on her return. From his behavior, it is very apparent that Dumuzi needs to spend some time in the underworld.

Emotion, compassion, and eros operate in Inanna's decree that Dumuzi and Geshtinanna will each spend half the year in the underworld. This is also true in the Demeter and Persephone myth. It ensures the cyclical nature of descent and return, and challenges the one-sided patriarchal conscious attitude that has ruled humankind for thousands of years. It follows the natural cycle of nature, where the seed rests in the ground for a period of time before it sprouts, grows into a plant, produces its fruit and seed, dies, and goes back into the earth for further transformation. We are also a part of nature and need to follow nature's rhythms. The result of this forgetfulness is our current global ecological crisis. Erishkigal will not turn into a monster like the Minotaur, devouring out of greed and grief, but she must be respected and honored for who she is and what she has to teach us.

What does the Inanna myth teach us about labyrinthine descent and return? She hears the call and makes a conscious decision to enter. She has a clear intention. She makes concrete, specific preparations. She has an ally in the upper world who will come to her rescue should she not return. In her preparation she also knows whose help to ask for (Enki's). She meets the guardian at the threshold. Her descent is slow and gradual and takes her through seven gates. She stays in the underworld for a period of time where its nature is integrated and absorbed, not destroyed. She comes to know the Goddess of the Underworld and suffers with her. The return brings its own perils and tasks, and Inanna now has both the wisdom and the ruthlessness with which to proceed.

The Healing Time

Finally on my way to yes
I bump into
all the places
where I said no
to my life
all the untended wounds
the red and purple scars
those hieroglyphs of pain
carved into my skin, my bones,
those coded messages
that send me down
the wrong street
again and again
when I find them
the old wounds
the old misdirections
and I lift them
one by one
close to my heart
and I say   holy
holy.[20]

—Pesha Gertler

20. From Marilyn Sewell, *Claiming the Spirit Within: A Sourcebook of Women's Poetry*, p. 319. Also published in *CrossCurrents, World Magazine,* and *Pontoon.* The poem has been set to music by Elizabeth Alexander, Ph.D., renamed "Finally on My Way to Yes," and will appear on CD in 2003 (available through Seafarer Press).

Dolls from Vassilisa workshop.

9

VASSILISA
THE BEAUTIFUL

I look at my face in the glass and see
A halfborn woman.[1]

—Adrienne Rich

The final goal of our intrepid, labyrinthine journey is to reconnect with the core of who we are and reclaim our inner power. The Russian fairy tale "Vassilisa the Beautiful" is another model for the journey. This time, the dark and the light meet, learn from each other, and are integrated successfully with each other and with the positive Masculine. This integration brings forth the power to act in the world in the service of the life-giving forces of the Feminine.

Here is the story. In a small village on the other side of the world lives a merchant with his eight-year-old daughter and his ailing wife. Knowing she does not have long to live, the mother calls over her beautiful daughter, Vassilisa, gives her a little doll,

1. Adrienne Rich, "Upper Broadway," in *The Dream of a Common Language*, p. 41.

and instructs her as follows: "Always keep this doll with you and if anything bad happens to you give it something to eat and ask its advice. It will first comfort you and then help you." Shortly thereafter, the mother dies.

The doll represents the compassionate, archetypal Feminine, in some sense, the energy of the Madonna I met in the cave. Connecting to compassion opens the doors to intuition. Vassilisa has been instructed about the necessity of having an ongoing relationship with her inner Feminine by spending time with her and feeding her. We do it by listening to our dreams, writing in journals, going for walks in the woods, or walking the labyrinth. Coming from a place of deep connection, we can endure whatever adversity comes our way and accomplish whatever tasks life sets out.

Vassilisa was eight years old when her mother died, as was Sarah when she had her how-dare-you experience. This is a time in a young girl's life when she begins to move beyond the confines of the protective environment of childhood and enters the larger cultural milieu. There is now a danger of her being disparaged for who she really is as the rules of society begin to take precedence. If she has not been given appropriate love and mirroring in her family, she may begin to doubt herself. With an ongoing relationship to her inner Feminine, Vassilisa remains intact.

Her father remarries a woman whom he thinks will be a good mother but who turns out to be the classical "wicked stepmother." The father represents an inner Masculine figure who means well but is not able to decipher the presence of negative Feminine energy. Part of us can be so caught up in patriarchal attitudes that we are blinded to what is right before our eyes. The stepmother and her daughters are jealous of Vassilisa, and do everything to subdue and minimize her. They are the energy of the Feminine ignored or betrayed. When a women is too frightened to allow her own life force to flow, she must kill it in everyone else. This is an integral component of the negative-mother complex which first happens to us externally with our real mothers in the world. We go on to absorb external negative attitudes toward the Feminine rampant in our culture, and then turn these negative attitudes against ourselves. They become internalized and it's hard to differentiate between what is true and untrue.

Throughout the tale, more and more abuse is heaped on Vassilisa. Each time this occurs, she goes into her little pantry, locks the door, and gives food to the doll (sometimes her entire rations of the day). The doll (intuitive knowing, and the part of Vassilisa bonded to her real mother), then accomplishes the ever increasing number of tasks for her.

As we get stronger, the ante is upped. In the fairy tale, the father goes away on an extended business trip, indicating that the Masculine exits from this part of the healing process. The stepmother moves her three daughters to a house closer to the woods (the unconscious) where Baba Yaga, the dark Feminine lives. They keep sending Vassilisa off, hoping she will meet her match and be killed. Then they too will be safe and at peace, for the story's boundaries will cease to be challenged by Vassilisa's aliveness. This does not happen. Vassilisa returns whole each time, with her connection to the doll intact.

Finally it is the time for Vassilisa to meet the dark Feminine for real. Until now she has been following the twists and turns of the labyrinth preparing for her time in the center. The stepmother orchestrates a situation in the house where all the lights go out and Vassilisa is sent by her stepsisters to Baba Yaga to get a new light (consciousness). When the eyes through which we see the world are no longer relevant, we are stuck. By spending time with the dark Feminine and learning what she has to teach, our vision is renewed and we move forward centered differently in ourselves.

Overwhelmed with dread, Vassilisa calls upon her doll, who tells her not to fear and to always keep her by her side. We must always stay connected to our loving, intuitive Feminine center. On her journey through the woods, Vassilisa sees a man clad in white on a white horse. Night gives way to dawn. Then she sees a man clad in red on a red horse. The sun begins to rise. Finally, at the end of the next day, Vassilisa arrives at Baba Yaga's hut. The fence around it is made of human bones and crowned with skulls, the gate is the bones of men's legs, the bolts are the bones of men's arms, and the lock is a set of sharp teeth. A third man rides by cloaked in black, on a black horse. As he gallops through the gate, night descends. This is the center where death resides.

Suddenly there is a great noise and Baba Yaga appears flying through the air in a wooden mortar swinging her pestle while announcing that she can smell Russian blood. Baba Yaga is the Goddess of All Nature, containing the power to give life and the power to annihilate. Baba Yaga is the Wild Woman, the Hag, and the Mistress of the Underworld personified.

Vassilisa says she has been sent by her stepsisters to get a light. This is the correct response, indicating Vassilisa is ready for the next step in her journey. Baba Yaga answers saying, yes, she knows this family well. Perhaps Vassilisa should enter, stay awhile, and work and they will see what can be seen. Baba Yaga knows all about the negative voices that destroy our Souls and is willing to provide Vassilisa with the space for her journey to continue. Using her magic, Baba Yaga opens the gate, they enter, and Vassilisa's initiation begins. She has knocked on the door and the guardian at the threshold has deemed her ready to continue.

The first thing Baba Yaga has Vassilisa do is to put all the food on the stove onto the table. Baba Yaga eats enough for ten people! The dark Feminine is voracious. Baba Yaga sets out Vassilisa's tasks for the first day. She is required to clean the yard, sweep the floor, cook the dinner, and take all the black bits out of the millet. If this is not done, Baba Yaga will eat her up. After Vassilisa feeds her doll and pours out her troubles, the doll replies, "Morning is wiser than evening." Sure enough, in the morning all the tasks are done. When Baba Yaga returns, she is surprised and calls on her servants to grind the millet. Three pairs of disembodied hands appear, take away the grain, and grind it. The next day, the same occurs, only this time Vassilisa must clean from each poppy seed the earth clinging to it.

The chores Vassilisa does for Baba Yaga are important; they are the inner tasks set for us during our time in the underworld. We need to clean, sweeping what has been hidden in dark corners into the light. We need to sort what is edible, what we can absorb and digest from what is indigestible. What thoughts and feelings about ourselves bear truth? What do we need to keep, and what to discard? We get to know this dark goddess by cooking for her, serving her food, living in her house, and being in her presence.

When Baba Yaga returns that evening, Vassilisa serves her dinner. Baba Yaga exclaims, "Don't stand there like a mute. Why don't you speak to me?" Vassilisa replies that she would like to ask a few questions. Baba Yaga's response is important. She says, "She who knows too much ages early," a warning that there are certain secrets of the dark not to be known to humans.

Vassilisa proceeds to ask her about the three horsemen she had seen. Baba Yaga responds saying that the White one is "my Bright Day," the Red is "my Radiant Sun," and the Black, "my Dark Night," indicating that Baba Yaga is the Mistress of Nature. Vassilisa asks nothing about the disembodied hands. Baba Yaga is pleased. She says she doesn't like people who are overly curious and that she eats them up. In her domain, we follow her rules. It is permissible to ask questions about what occurs outside the house, but we are forbidden to ask about what occurs in the inner sanctum of the dark Feminine (this part of the mystery is forbidden and dangerous for humans to know).

Baba Yaga asks Vassilisa how she got all the tasks done on time. Vassilisa replies "with the help of something my mother gave me." Here the two powers face each other. Vassilisa, with the power of the loving, intuitive Feminine in the form of the doll; Baba Yaga with the power of the dark night and the relentlessness of nature. They have gained a mutual respect for each other through their interactions. Baba Yaga sends Vassilisa off, saying people like her, connected to the loving Feminine and able to find their way in the dark, have no business being here at all. She hands Vassilisa an illuminated skull on a stick to take back to her stepsisters.

Vassilisa returns home, carrying with her the power of what she has learned in the dark place, symbolized by the lighted skull. She finds her house in darkness, because no light would stay lit since her departure. She is greeted by her stepmother and stepsisters. The eyes of the skull, Vassilisa's ability to see with new insight, focus on the stepmother and stepsisters who try desperately to escape. Over the course of the night, they are burned to cinders.

It is important to burn away the negativity we have inherited, cultivated, and nourished ourselves with. Negative thoughts can be fed, embellished, aggrandized, used as weapons against ourselves and others, and as justification for our lack of success in life. Negativity only breeds further negativity. Negativity is not done away with instantly; it is a slow process. In the healing process, we need to ask ourselves: "Given who we are today, is this thought I am carrying around about myself, about my life, about life in general really true, or is it a carryover from times past?" "Are these negative thoughts trying to give me a message about what I am doing here and now?" "What am I gaining by staying in this negative state?" We play games with ourselves, both consciously and unconsciously, and it drains us of both time and energy. The fire burning in the skull's eyes knows death and sees what is true. Our negativity will slowly diminish as we pay it less and less heed.

When Vassilisa awakens in the morning (becomes conscious and is ready to move on), she locks up the house and goes to live with an old woman she knows. Vassilisa is now able to be in the presence of a different kind of Feminine and needs time for integration and healing. This is the journey out of the center of the labyrinth.

After some time, Vassilisa gets bored and asks for some flax, which the woman brings to her. At this time in a woman's life creativity can flourish, for she now has courage and clear vision and can dare to risk being herself. She is no longer satisfied with the old. Vassilisa spins yarn that is fine and beautiful. When she is ready to weave it into cloth, no loom can be found. With the help of her doll (her intuition), she is able to fashion the perfect loom for this special thread. Weaving cloth symbolizes the combining of aspects of life into a new fabric.

Vassilisa creates the most beautiful cloth, and instructs the old woman to sell it and keep the money for herself. The old woman gives it to the tzar as a gift. He tries to get someone to sew it but no one has a needle fine enough. He asks the old woman to do it and she tells him about Vassilisa. He sends the fabric back. Vassilisa works all night until she has sewn twelve shirts, which she then sends back to the tzar. He is so pleased that he wants to meet the woman who has sewn them. When the tzar sees Vassilisa for the first time, he falls in love with her and asks her to marry him. She does. Her father comes back from his travels and moves in with them, as does the old woman with whom she has been living. This symbolizes an integration of the Masculine and Feminine aspects of the personality, and a gathering of creative energy in order to step forward into life.

Vassilisa now has eyes that see forward and backward into truth, and has integrated this seeing into her whole being. She is ready to move out into the world as an intact, undivided person with an intuitive Feminine and an active Masculine that work in sync with each other rather than in discord. This is the ultimate goal of our descent and return from the underworld, the desired result of the labyrinth journey.

> I refuse to become a seeker for cures.
> Everything that has ever
> helped me has come through what already
> lay stored in me. Old things, diffuse, untamed, lie strong
> across my heart.
> This is from where
> my strength comes, even when I miss my strength
> even when it turns on me
> like a violent master.[2]
> —*Adrienne Rich*

---

2. Adrienne Rich, " Sources II," in *Your Native Land Your Life*, p. 4.

EPILOGUE

Our deepest fear is not that we are inadequate.
Our deepest fear is that we are powerful beyond measure. It
is our light not our darkness that most frightens us. . . . And
as we let our own light shine, we unconsciously give other
people permission to do the same. As we are liberated from
our fear, our presence automatically liberates others.[1]

—Nelson Mandela

Strong is what we make
each other. Until we are all strong together,
a strong woman is a woman strongly afraid.[2]

—Marge Piercy

We have traveled far together. Through the labyrinth, we have
grounded ourselves in the ancient caves of the Goddess, and in
profound Feminine wisdom extending from that time to the present. We have learned about the journey we must undertake in

1. Nelson Mandela, 1994 Inaugural Speech.
2. Marge Piercy, "For strong women," *Circles on the Water.*

order to meet Her, that part of ourselves, in all its splendor and anguish. We have learned much about her multidimensionality and how she mirrors us back to ourselves. We have seen what happens when she is ignored. Through myths and fairy tales we have looked at some of the archetypal patterns that inform the journey and deepen our understanding.

Most important we have learned that pain is a valuable teacher. We must not hang on to it like a precious jewel nor run from it in terror. We must allow pain to flow through us, touching us deeply, keeping our hearts open and our compassion flowing to ourselves and others. Being grounded in pain—not just personal pain, but the pain of being alive and human, and sharing this planet with other creatures—allows us to see the world through different eyes. We can no longer hate; we are united through our shared humanity. Knowing the other's pain and resonating to that pain in ourselves breaks down barriers that divide and creates an ocean of compassion in which we can all float. Being grounded in pain is the route to experiencing profound joy.

The labyrinth is our container for this. It holds us as we move through life giving us the sense that we are a part of something much larger, mysterious, magical, and profound than we as human beings can ever know. The labyrinth is a symbol for the unconditional love that is our birthright. Its message for us each time we engage with it, in whatever form we choose, is to remember this. When we begin to live our lives from this knowing, we will change the world.

> Yet if I could instruct
> myself, if we could learn to learn from pain
> even as it grasps us   if the mind, the mind that lives
> in this body could refuse   to let itself be crushed
> in that grasp   it would loosen   Pain would have to stand
> off from me and listen   its dark breath still on me
> but the mind would begin to speak to pain
> and pain would have to answer:[3]
>   —*Adrienne Rich*

3. Adrienne Rich, "Splittings," *The Dream of a Common Language*, p. 10.

The Challenge

It is time to wake up, to throw off the yoke of our patriarchal vision, and see with eyes that know the color, texture, scent, and juiciness of the dark. The Feminine beckons us to meet her, to journey through her vast intimacy, to come alive with her knowing, to tremble with the vigor of her life force, to bask in the gentleness of her charismatic loving. Her profound question to us, one we *must* respond to is, "Who do we serve?"

Are we serving false gods—wealth, comfort, conformity, somnambulance, fear, judgment, addiction? Answering this question is not simple. We become so easily habituated to a way of being that we lose sight of possible choices. We can sleepwalk through our days feeling dead, helpless, and hopeless, or party through our nights in a manic gesture to feel alive, while underneath there may be a being writhing in pain, cowering in fear, swimming in despair, smouldering in rage. What we serve in this case is anything to keep us from our authenticity, from embracing all of who we are, both the light and the dark.

The Feminine summons us. She is saying, "Listen, I will hold you in love. Listen, I will create a safe space where you can meet yourself again. Listen, and you will know the community of others who are journeying to meet me, know me, live from me. Listen, and you will no longer be alone. Listen, as your aliveness begins to blossom and your power infuses you. Listen, and you will step forth into life in a new way."

Through the labyrinth the Feminine is calling us to serve her values of love, truth, and beauty. She wants us to honor the sanctity of all life above all else, and to act in the world from a place of fierce compassion. She teaches us that anger breeds anger, hatred breeds hatred, and murder breeds revenge. But love and compassion breed more love and compassion. As I follow the news in these potent days of conflict on our planet and read about how mutual loathing is being fueled by propaganda, and how each act of violence brings about retaliation, I pray that more of us become convinced that war is not the answer, but the problem.

When I was very young, I remember hearing my parents speak

about war and about the United Nations. I understood that this was a gathering of all the important people from all the countries in the world, and their purpose was to make sure no big wars ever happened again. It seemed they were not succeeding. I spent hours fantasizing that I would one day go to speak to these important men at the United Nations and say, "War is Stupid. You must be stupid, too, if you keep having wars, so stop it right now! Stop killing babies! You need to love everyone!" I was convinced that if they just knew the truth they would stop. I thought no one had ever told them before.

I have looked back over those fantasies with a kind of patronizing indulgence at my naiveté, but also awed by my precocity. We think we are so complex and have developed theories to explain everything: psychology, religion, history, economics, and politics. We are deluged with information and sometimes it feels like we are drowning in words. At the core, there are some very simple truths. I knew them when I was young and I sense many young children know them now, but we forget. It is time to remember.

Many are remembering. In Canada we have the Raging Grannies. In South America we have the Mothers of the Disappeared. In Britain they are called Hell's Grannies—Women in Black. The Women in Black, mostly middle-aged and elderly are taking a remarkable stand in the current Middle East crisis. They have traveled to Jerusalem and moved into Palestinian houses, ensuring that if the Israelis try to attack innocent civilians they will also be attacking them. They are teaching Palestinians about nonviolent protest. They stand at checkpoints as observers, putting their own lives at risk. They are true Heroines. Women in Black inspire and challenge us with their courage. If they can, why can't we?

Women in the Peace Process

Here is an example of what happens when women join together in an effort to create peace. Bat Shalom is an organization of Palestinian and Israeli women created in spite of the tremendous opposition to any camaraderie between the two sides. On May 7, 2002, their director, Terry Greenblatt, gave a speech at the UN. The following is an excerpt from that talk. It speaks clearly of why women must be involved in the peace process and what we have to contribute.

You need us, because if the goal is not simply the absence of war, but the creation of a sustainable peace by fostering fundamental societal changes, we are crucial to everyone's security concerns.

You need us, because wars are no longer fought on battlefields. You have brought the war home to us. Many more civilians than soldiers are being killed in ours and other conflicts around the world. The wars are being waged now on our doorsteps and in our living rooms and in our sacred houses and ceremonies of religious worship, and women have a vested interest in keeping families and communities safe.

You need us because we continue to hold human rights and the sanctity of life as paramount values, and unfortunately today, they are too easily being bartered away as either obstacles to security policies or as incongruent with national liberation aspirations.

You need us because we have developed a process and sociopolitical fluency that keeps authentic and productive dialogue moving forward, even as the violence escalates and both sides continue to terrorize one another. Women's characteristic life experience gives us the potential for two things: a very special kind of intelligence, social intelligence, and a very special kind of courage, social courage. We have developed the courage to cross the lines of difference drawn between us, which are also the lines drawn inside our heads. And the intelligence to do it safely, without a gun or a bomb, and to do it productively. And most importantly, we are learning to shift our positions, finding ourselves moving towards each other, without tearing out our roots in the process. Even when we are women whose very existence and narrative contradicts each other, we will talk—we will not shoot.

You need us because we women are willing to sit together on the same side of the table and together look at our complex joint history, with the commitment and intention of not getting up until—in respect and reciprocity—we can get up together and begin our new history and fulfill our joint destiny.

We need to join together in community grounded in simple truths. Pain is our teacher, not our enemy. Love and compassion for all is our goal. To create a world where people have the opportunity to become wholly who they are is what we are striving for. Women need to reach out to and receive each other, simultaneously keening our grief and dancing our joy. We need to raise our voices. We need to know what we must say Yes to and what we must say No to, and do it. Singly, collectively, it makes no difference. It is time for each of us to journey to our center to answer the question of who we serve. Time is short. Our planet is failing. Our only choice is to find our voices and live from a place of integrity, love, and fierce compassion.

> But there come times—perhaps this is one of them—
> when we have to take ourselves more seriously or die;
> when we have to pull back from the incantations,
> rhythms we've moved to thoughtlessly
> and disenthrall ourselves[4]
>
> We shrink from touching
> our power, we shrink away, we starve ourselves
> and each other, we're scared shitless
> of what it could be to take and use our love,
> hose it on a city, on a world,
> to wield and guide its spray, destroying
> poisons, parasites, rats, viruses—
> like the terrible mothers we long and dread to be.[5]

---

4. Adrienne Rich, "Transcendental Etude," *The Dream of a Common Language*, pp. 74–75.
5. Adrienne Rich, "Hunger," *The Dream of a Common Language*, p. 13.

My heart is moved by all I cannot save:
so much has been destroyed
I have to cast my lot with those
who age after age, persevere,
with no extraordinary power to
reconstitute the world.[6]
                    —*Adrienne Rich*

6. Adrienne Rich, "Natural Resources," *The Dream of a Common Language*, p. 67.

BIBLIOGRAPHY

Attali, Jacques. *The Labyrinth in Culture and Society: Pathways to Wisdom*. Berkeley, CA: North Atlantic Books, 1999.

Baker, Carolyn. *Reclaiming the Dark Feminine: The Price of Desire*. Tempe, AZ: New Falcon Publications,1996.

Baring, Anne, and Jules Cashford. *The Myth of the Goddess: Evolution of an Image*. London: Arkana, Penguin Books, 1993.

Boer, Charles. *The Homeric Hymns: The Charles Boer Translation*. Dallas, TX: Spring Publications, 1970.

Bord, Janet. *Mazes and Labyrinths of the World*. London: Latimer New Dimensions Ltd., 1976.

Campbell, Joseph. *The Hero With a Thousand Faces*. Bollingen Series XVII. Princeton: Princeton University Press, 1949.

Conty, Patrick. "The Geometry of the Labyrinth," *Parabola,* Volume XVII, Number 2, May 1992.

Darroch-Lozowski, Vivian. "Initiation in Hermeneutics: An illustration through the mother-and-daughter archetype," *Human Studies* 13: 237–251, Netherlands: Kluwer Academic Publishers, 1990.

Deedes, C. N., "The Labyrinth," *The Labyrinth—Further Studies in the Relation between Myth and Ritual in the Ancient World,* edited by S. H. Hooke. New York: The Macmillan Company, 1935.

Doob, Penelope Reed. *The Idea of the Labyrinth—from Classical Antiquity Through the Middle Ages*. Ithaca and London: Cornell University Press, 1990.

Douglas, Claire. *Translate This Darkness: The Life of Christiana Morgan—The Veiled Woman in Jung's Circle*. New York: Simon and Schuster, 1993.

Douglas, Claire. *Visions: Notes of the Seminar Given in 1930–1934 by C. G. Jung*. Bollingen Series XCIX. Princeton: Princeton University Press, 1997.

Eliade, Mircea. *Images and Symbols: Studies in Religious Symbolism*. Princeton: Princeton University Press, 1991.

Eliade, Mircea. *Myths, Dreams, and Mysteries*. New York: Harper and Row, 1957.

Eliade, Mircea. *Rites and Symbols of Initiation: The Mysteries of Birth and Rebirth.* New York: Harper and Row, 1958.

Galland, China. *The Bond Between Women: A Journey to Fierce Compassion.* New York: Riverhead Books, 1998.

Gimbutas, Marija. *The Goddesses and Gods of Old Europe—Myths and Cult Images.* Berkeley: University of California Press, 1982.

Gimbutas, Marija. *The Language of the Goddess.* San Francisco: Harper Collins Publishers, 1989.

Gleick, James. *Chaos—Making a New Science.* New York: Penguin Books, 1987.

Harman, Willis, and Howard Rheingold. *Higher Creativity: Liberating the Unconscious for Breakthrough Insights.* Los Angeles: Jeremy P. Tarcher, 1984.

Houston, Jean. *The Search for the Beloved.* Los Angeles: Jeremy P. Tarcher, Inc., 1987.

Johnson, Buffie. *Lady of the Beasts: Ancient Images of the Goddess and Her Sacred Animals.* San Francisco: Harper and Row, 1988.

Jung, C. G. *Collected Works,* vol. 5. London: Routledge and Kegan Paul. 1956.

Jung, C. G. *Collected Works,* vol. 8. London: Routledge and Kegan Paul, 1960.

Jung, C. G. *Collected Works,* vol. 9i. London: Routledge and Kegan Paul, 1959.

Jung, C. G. *Collected Works,* vol. 13. London: Routledge and Kegan Paul, 1968.

Jung, C. G., and K. Kerenyi. *Essays on a Science of Mythology: The Myth of the Divine Child and the Mysteries of Eleusis.* Bollingen Series XXII. Princeton: Princeton University Press, 1949.

Kerenyi, Karl. *Eleusis, Archetypal Image of Mother and Daughter.* Bollingen Series LXV. vol. 4. Princeton: Princeton University Press, 1962.

Knight, W. F. Jackson. *Cumean Gates—A Reference of the Sixth Aeneid to the Initiation Pattern.* Oxford: Basil Blackwell, 1936.

Layard, John. "The Malekulan Journey of the Dead," *Eranos Yearbooks,* Bollingen XXX vol. 4. Princeton: Princeton University Press, 1960.

Levy, Gertrude Rachel. *The Gate of Horn: A Study of the Religious Conceptions of the Stone Age, and Their Influence upon European Thought.* London: Faber and Faber Limited, 1946.

Lincoln, Bruce. *Emerging from the Chrysalis—Studies in Rituals of Women's Initiation*. Cambridge, MA: Harvard University Press, 1981.

Mathew, W. H. *Mazes and Labyrinths: A General Account of Their History and Development*. London: Longmans, Green and Co., 1922.

McLean, Adam. *The Triple Goddess—An Exploration of the Archetypal Feminine*. Grand Rapids, MI: Phanes Press, 1989.

McPherson, Sigrid R. *The Refiner's Fire: Memoirs of a German Girlhood*. Toronto: Inner City Books, 1992.

Meador, Betty De Shong. *Uncursing the Dark—Treasures from the Underworld*. Wilmette, IL: Chiron Publications, 1992.

Meador, Betty De Shong. *Inanna: Lady of Largest Heart / Poems of the Sumerian High Priestess Enheduanna*. Austin: University of Texas Press, 2000.

Miller, Malcolm. *Chartres Cathedral*. Pitkin: North Way, Andover, Hants, 1980.

Otto, Walter F. "The Meaning of the Eleusinian Mysteries," *Eranos Yearbook XXX*. New York: Bollingen Foundation, 1955.

O'Kane, Francoise. *Sacred Chaos. Reflections on God's Shadow and the Dark Self*. Toronto: Inner City Books, 1994.

Perera, Sylvia Brinton. *Descent to the Goddess—A Way of Initiation for Women*. Toronto: Inner City Books, 1981.

Ruiz, Don Miguel. *The Four Agreements: A Toltec Wisdom Book*. San Rafael, CA: Amber-Allen Publishing, 1997.

Scully, Vincent. *The Earth, The Temple, and The Gods—Greek Sacred Architecture*. New Haven and London: Yale University Press, revised edition 1979.

Sullivan, Barbara Stevens. *Psychotherapy Grounded in the Feminine Principle*. Wilmette, IL: Chiron Publications, 1989.

Tarrant, John. *The Light Inside the Dark*. New York: HarperCollins, 1998.

Walker, Barbara G. *The Woman's Dictionary of Symbols and Sacred Objects*. San Francisco: Harper and Row, 1988.

Whitmont, Edward C. *The Symbolic Quest—Basic Concepts of Analytical Psychology*. Princeton: Princeton University Press, 1969.

Wolkstein, Diane, and Samuel Noah Kramer. *Inanna, Queen of Heaven and Earth*. New York: Harper and Row, 1983.

Woodman, Marion, and Elinor Dickson. *Dancing in the Flames: The Dark Goddess in the Transformation of Consciousness*. New York: Shambhala, 1996.

Poetry and Literature

Clarke, Lindsay. *Alice's Masque*. London: Picador, 1994.

Hirshfield, Jane. *The October Palace*, NY: HarperCollins, 1994.

Lindsay, Jayelle. *Tangible Evidence: A Book of Poems*. Schneckli Press, Guelph, ON, 1998.

Moyne, John, and Coleman Barks. *Unseen Rain: Quatrains of Rumi*. Watsonville, CA: Threshold Books, 1986.

Piercy, Marge. *Circles on the Water*. New York: Knopf, 1994.

Purce, Jill. *The Mystic Spiral—Journey of the Soul*. New York: Avon, 1974.

Rich, Adrienne. *The Dream of a Common Language*. New York: Norton, 1994.

Rich, Adrienne. *Your Native Land Your Life*. New York: Norton, 1986.

Sewell, Marilyn, ed. *Claiming the Spirit Within: A Sourcebook of Women's Poetry*. Boston: Beacon Press, 1996.

Welwood, Jennifer Paine. *Poems for the Path*. 1998, 1999. P.O. Box 2173, Mill Valley, CA 94942.

INDEX

addiction, 64, 70, 102, 146, 183
Aeneid, 42
Aigeus, King, 128, 130
alchemists, 37
Alexander, Elizabeth, 170
Allen, Woody, 70
allies, 66, 71–73, 136, 169
ancestors, 2, 4, 19, 33, 34, 46
Aphrodite, 51, 53, 55, 129, 131
archetype, 4, 5, 20–23, 42, 58, 64, 94, 123, 136
Ariadne, 20, 40, 129, 136
Artress, Lauren, 5
Attali, Jacques, 1
Avendon, Richard, 49
axe, 19, 20

Baba Yaga, 75, 94, 175–177
Baker, Carolyn, 98–99
Baring, Anne, 159
Barks, Coleman, 25, 119, 151
Bat Shalom, 184
beast, 55, 77, 88, 134, 135
birth, 1, 8, 10, 17, 36, 38, 39, 40, 41, 55, 87, 94, 95, 144
Black Madonna, 52, 55, 97
blood, 113, 114, 128, 134, 157, 163, 166, 176
Boer, Charles, 140
brain, 5, 39
bull, 20, 40, 129, 131, 156, 159
Burns, Melinda, 102–103

call, 66, 71–73, 162, 164, 169
Campbell, Joseph, 66
Cashford, Jules, 159
cave(s), 9, 15, 16, 17, 20, 64, 86, 88, 94, 95, 96, 107, 144, 181
chakra(s), 6, 56–57, 57, 164
Chaos, 2, 3, 22, 23–24, 34, 41, 68, 154
Charpentier, Louis, 52
Chartres, *ii*, 4, 11, 45, *48*, 49–52, 60, 164
  -style labyrinth, 17, 19, 20
Christian, 42, 45, 50, 51, 52, 55,
Clark, Lindsay, 78, 85
Clement of Alexandria, 145
conjunctio, 36, 148
conscious(ness), 21, 32, 35, 43, 44, 56, 62, 78, 80, 83, 86, 87, 110, 115, 123, 134, 135, 140, 143, 145, 148, 163, 175, 178
container, 2, 28–32, 37, 136, 163, 182
Conty, Patrick, 53–54
Crane Dance, 42
Crete, 16, 19–20, 128, 129, 133, 140, 141
  -style labyrinth, 17, 19, 20, 42

Crone, 143

Daedelus, 129
dakini, 107, 108
dance, 4, 7, 8, 16, 21, 23, 24, 27, 35, 42, 44, 64, 65, 77, 86, 87, 108, 167, 186
Dark Goddess, 75, 143, 150
Darroch-Lozowski, Vivian, 38
death, 1, 8, 17, 32, 34, 37, 38, 40, 41, 42, 46, 55, 65, 66, 73, 75, 94, 95, 97, 99, 107, 127, 134, 143, 146, 156, 160, 164, 165, 169, 176
Deedes, C. N., 46
Demeter, 11, 91, 123, *138*, 139–151
depression, 2, 58, 62, 74, 76, 145, 164
descent, 61, 64, 65, 71, 75, 77, 112, 123, 128, 130, 159, 169
Dionysus, 129
dissociation, 70, 76, 117
Doob, Penelope Reed, 22
Douglas, Claire, 8, 118
dream(s), 1, 2, 3, 21, 31, 43, 64, 85, 100, 103, 111, 112, 115, 148, 162, 174
Dromenon, 4
Durga, 75, 94
Durrenmatt, Friedrich, 126
Druid(s), 4, 51, 144

Ego, 44, 109, 163
Eleusis, 44, 141
Eleusinian Mysteries, 150, 159
Eliade, Mircea, 15, 27, 37–38, 41, 58
Enki, 147, 151, 168, 169
Eros, 130, 133, 169
Erishkigal, 40, 111, 159, 168
Evans, Sir Arthur, 19
evil, 42, 62, 66, 69, 81, 109, 110, 111, 153, 166, 168
extroversion, 29, 32, 70

fairy tale, 11, 21, 65, 76, 123, 173, 175
falling, 105–107
feces, 117, 149, 166
Feminine, 1, 9, 11, 16, 19, 20, 22, 23, 27, 32, 33, 43, 46, 51, 55, 56, 62, 67, 85, 86, 88, 95, 102, 104, 105, 112–113, 127, 130, 133, 146, 150, 167, 173, 179, 183
  Dark/dark, 8, 58, 86, 90, 91, 95, 98, 100, 104, 163, 175
  deplored, 110
  energy, 2, 8, 16, 30, 62, 99, 100, 118
  Divine, 9, 10, 55, 94–97
  ignored, 98–102, 174
  nature, 3

power, 3
Primordial, 9, 10, 77, 86–90, 91, 95
wounded, 63, 68, 91, 105, 112
fierce compassion, 9, 75, 108, 109, 183, 186
Fierz David, Linda, 8, 86, 87, 90
Findhorn, Scotland, 29
fire, 30, 37, 51, 97, 142, 178
flying, 111, 176
four, 55–56
freemasonry, 52

Gaia, 140
Galland, China, 108
Gertler, Pesha, 170
Gleick, James, 22–23, 24
God, 32, 43, 51, 68, 72, 74, 107, 110, 135
Goddess, 1, 9, 16, 20, 33, 43, 52, 55, 64,
    83, 86, 94, 97, 116, 132, 133, 139, 154,
    159, 181
Grace Cathedral (San Francisco), 5
Great Mother, 17, 20, 21, 39, 130, 132
Greenblatt, Terry, 184, 185–186
guardian, 66, 71–73, 133, 135, 164, 169,
    176
guilt, 33, 82, 92, 101, 104, 109, 112, 160

Hades, 130, 141, 143
Hag, 70, 75, 76, 94, 176
Hannah, Barbara, 8
Harman, Willis, 52
healing, 22, 30, 31, 39, 64, 65, 66, 68, 69,
    79, 83, 94, 97, 100, 113, 116, 117, 147,
    151, 166, 175, 178
Hecate, 138, 141, 144
Hero, 24, 66, 67, 75, 117, 123, 127, 128,
    130, 164
Hirshfield, Jane, 137
Homer, 42
Houston, Jean, 3, 4, 5, 7, 29
Human Capacities program, 3, 5

Iliad, 42
Inanna, 11, 40, 66, 71, 74, 75, 76, 91, 111,
    124, 140, 147, 151, 152, 152–170
individuation, 5, 40, 71
inertia, 86, 90, 91–94, 146, 164
initiation, 15, 37, 38, 41, 56, 58, 65, 83,
    118, 131, 150, 176
inner child, 45, 67, 75, 79, 80
inner demons, 62, 95, 146
introversion, 29, 32, 70
intuition, 8, 39, 56, 73, 144, 174, 175, 177,
    178
Iraq, 110, 153

Jerusalem, 90, 43, 184
John of the Cross, 74
Johnson, Buffie, 55
Joyce, Dianne, 63, 83, 97–98
Jung, C.G., 5, 19, 20, 23, 24, 32, 34–35, 37,
    40, 53, 56, 61, 68, 82, 86, 109, 118,
    139

Jung Institute, 8, 29

Kabbalah, 153
Kali, 75, 94
karma, 33, 36
Kerenyi, Karl, 45, 139
King, Martin Luther, 103
Knight, Jackson, 37, 42
Knossos, 19, 44
Kramer, Samuel Noah, 153, 161, 165
Kuan Yin, 94
Kundalini, 92

labyrinth,
    –building, 9
    –center, 4, 10, 16, 25, 31, 34, 38, 40, 41,
        44, 50, 53, 57, 66, 71, 74–76, 80, 81,
        123, 133, 146, 164
    –eleven-circuit, ii, xiv, 17, 19, 20, 39
    –history, 51
    –quadrant, 16, 53, 55, 74, 164
    –seven-circuit, 17, 19, 20
    –walking, 2, 5, 8, 9, 10, 15, 29, 31, 33,
        36, 38, 43, 53, 164
Layard, John, 17
Le-Hev-Hev, 17, 23, 26, 75
Lincoln, Bruce, 145
Lindsay, Jayelle, 77
Luce, Gay, 3

madness, 76, 132, 135, 163
Maat, 7
Madonna, *84*, 94, 97, 98, 107, 174
Maiden, 143
Malekula, 17, 23, 26, 75
Mandela, Nelson, 181
Masculine, 16, 112, 147, 163, 173, 174,
    179
    -energy, 8, 91
Masters, Bob, 3
maze, 23, 42, 79
McLean, Adam, 148
McVeigh, Timothy, 110
Meador, Betty DeShong, 153, 155–158
Medicine Wheel, 94
Miller, Malcolm, 51
Minos, King, 128
Minotaur, 11, 40, 123, *126*, 127–134, 164,
    164
monster, 40, 66, 128, 131, 134, 169
moon, 20, 25, 31, 33, 131, 132, 144
    -phase, 34
Morgan, Christiana, 118
mother, 3, 7, 20–21, 55, 62, 68,87, 91,
    139, 143, 186
    good enough, 68, 69
    negative, 82, 99, 100, 124, 174
Mother Earth, 3, 15, 16, 52
Moyne, John, 25, 119, 151
myth, 5, 11, 21, 40, 65, 67, 123, 139, 162

narcissus, 140, 143

Norris, Kathleen, 127

O'Kane, Francoise, 167
Odysssey, 58
opus, 2, 37

Paleolithic, 16, 33
paradox, 41, 88, 95, 154, 158
patriarchy, 43, 62, 87, 99, 128, 132, 140, 145, 148, 165, 169, 174, 183
Pelli, 97
Perera, Sylvia Brinton, 168
Persephone, 11, 71, 91, 123, *138*, 139–151
Piercy, Marge, 181
poison, 81, 90, 99, 110, 128, 130, 134, 155, 186
pomegranate, 142, 147
Poseidon, 128
progression, 32, 33, 53, 79
psyche, 4, 19, 38, 54, 55, 88, 118, 136
psychodrama, 134, 143

Quinlan, Barb, 32

rape, 71, 73, 123, 143, 151
Red Madonna, 97
regression, 32, 33, 53, 64, 67, 68, 69, 71, 79, 151
Rich, Adrienne, 8, 173, 179, 182, 186–187
ring, 115, 129
ritual, 2, 4, 5, 15, 17, 30, 33, 37, 42, 44, 58, 114, 150
Ruiz, Don Miguel, 80–83
Rumi, 25, 119, 151

sacred space, 4, 30, 32, 37, 38, 134
Scully, Vincent, 44
Self, 35, 40, 45, 57, 63, 68, 115
seven, 53, 56, 129, 159, 160, 164, 169
Sewell, Marilyn, 170
sexual, 2, 55, 87, 165
  abuse, 69
  humor, 146
shadow, 106, 128, 133, 165
  collective, 109
  personal, 95, 110, 111
shaman(ic) 41, 65, 101
sin, 55, 56
six, 55
skull, 175, 177
snake, 4, 42–43, 158, 162
Sophia, 94, 153
sorrow, 6, 7, 32, 58, 74, 75, 83, 105–109, 133, 167
Soul, 11, 21, 28, 29, 31, 32, 36, 40, 63, 71, 87, 106, 143, 148, 176

spider, 99–100
Spirit, 28–29, 30, 31, 32, 37, 40, 63, 65, 68, 71, 75, 105, 106
splitting, 70, 76
Sumer(ia), 40, 124, 140, 152, 153
sword, 128, 132, 135
symbol, 27–28
synchronicity, 21, 29, 71

Tao, 5
Tarrant, John, 28, 74
temenos, 37, 38, 164
Theseus, 11, 20, 40, 66, 71, 123, 127–134, 163
transformation, 23, 37, 38, 41, 54, 55, 64, 66, 123, 130, 133, 136, 163, 169
Triple Goddess, *138*, 140, 142, 143, 147, 148, 150
true self, 68, 70

Ulysses, 58
unbearable anxiety, 68, 71, 76
unconscious, 21, 39, 66, 96, 103, 109, 112, 114, 130, 131, 133, 181
underworld, 37, 41, 64, 65, 71, 73, 74, 123, 130, 140, 142, 147, 154, 159, 164, 167, 175, 176, 178
unicursal, 22, 44
United Nations, 184

Van Doren, Robin, 3
Vassilisa, 11, 124, 172, 173–179
Virgil, 42
voice, 3, 9, 10, 36, 63, 73, 85, 93, 102–105, 119, 150, 166, 186

Walker, Barbara, 55
war, 42, 90, 110, 142, 183, 185
Welwood, Jennifer, 108
Wild Woman, 176
wisdom, 1, 43, 56, 65, 86, 94, 181
Whitmont, Edward, 86, 87
Winnicott, W. D., 68, 69, 70
witch, 31, 36, 75, 94, 130, 165
Wolkenstein, Diane, 153, 161, 165
Woodman, Marion, 7, 82
womb, 20, 38, 44, 87, 144, 159
Women in Black, 184
wounded child, 67, 75, 80, 81

yin energy, 86, 88, 89, 90
yoga, 31, 32

Zachariah, Lois, 105–107
Zeus, 130, 141
Zurich, 3, 5, 8, 29, 30, 86, 100